Praise for The ... People
Don't Want to Hear

"In a time of division and heightened rhetoric, the task of preaching can seem perilous, especially preaching on sensitive and challenging issues. Lisa Cressman does not shrink from the task. She takes into account the complex context of listeners and creatively describes a way of preaching that is prophetically faithful and an act of deep pastoral care."

Thomas G. Long, Bandy Professor Emeritus of Preaching, Candler School of Theology

"Lisa Cressman's book comes at just the right time for helping preachers guide their congregations through inevitable change and upheaval. With her characteristic creativity and candor, Cressman fearlessly addresses the anxieties of clergy and churches while providing gospel-centered, practical, and hope-filled ideas for navigating this challenging time. Her trust in the ever-renewing love of God is contagious!"

Leah D. Schade, author of *Preaching in the Purple Zone: Ministry in the Red-Blue Divide*

"Lisa Cressman invites us to courageously live into the chaotic realities of our falling skies so that we may fully participate with God in the creation of something new. This text will be a trusted companion for those who find themselves having to preach through the uncertainties of life."

Mark Andrew Jefferson, Assistant Professor of Homiletics, Virginia Theological Seminary

"In this book Lisa Cressman rightly names the rigorous and dangerous challenge preachers face as they enter the pulpit to preach an unflinching gospel message. Reading her words feels like sitting with a friend whom you know understands this lonely, risky work. For use in personal reflection or with a community of praxis, this guide will help you deepen and enrich your preaching and the spiritual practice that informs it."

Amy Butler, pastor, leader, teacher, writer

"This book is a timely call for preachers to proclaim the timeless Gospel. Lisa Cressman shows us how to preach with the power of faith instead of fear and to lead our congregations toward transformative discipleship instead of entrenched division."

Micah Jackson, president, Bexley Seabury Seminary

THE GOSPEL
PEOPLE DON'T
WANT TO HEAR

THE GOSPEL PEOPLE DON'T WANT TO HEAR

Preaching Challenging Messages

LISA CRESSMAN

Fortress Press
Minneapolis

THE GOSPEL PEOPLE DON'T WANT TO HEAR
Preaching Challenging Messages

Copyright © 2020 by Lisa Cressman. Published by Fortress Press, an imprint of 1517 Media. All rights reserved. Except for brief quotations in critical articles or reviews, no part of this book may be reproduced in any manner without prior written permission from the publisher. Email copyright@1517.media or write to Permissions, Fortress Press, PO Box 1209, Minneapolis, MN 55440-1209.

Cover design: Emily Harris Designs
Typesetting: PerfecType, Nashville, TN

Print ISBN: 978-1-5064-5639-3
eBook ISBN: 978-1-5064-5640-9

TABLE OF CONTENTS

"The sky is falling! The sky is falling!"
That's what we hear *ad infinitum, ad nauseam*:
"It's all falling apart!
It's spinning out of control!
It's the end of the world!
The sky is falling! The sky is falling!"
I'm not here to tell you otherwise. The sky *is* falling.
Let it.
(That's the gospel people don't want to hear.)

INTRODUCTION

Let's imagine a cruise ship christened *The Mother Ship Earth* on which you have booked an extended trip. You walk the gang-plank into *The Mother Ship Earth* and are greeted by your cruise director. She welcomes you sincerely and asks on which side of the ship you wish your berth to be: the politically conservative side of the ship, or the liberal side? You're surprised by the question, but you're on vacation. You want to relax. You're tired of dealing with the people who would select the other side, so you select the side akin to your views. "Very good," she says and continues, "what evening dining time do you prefer? 7:00? Perfect."

She goes on, "As to dining at 7:00, do you wish to dine in the dining rooms set aside for those from your side of the ship, or are you open to a dining room with mixed political company?" Now you feel a bit embarrassed. You don't want to appear closed-minded (what would Jesus say, after all?), so you say you're willing to sit in the mixed dining room. With that decided, the director asks whether you prefer to sit at one of few remaining seats available at one of the "politics *off* the table" tables, or have a seat at one of the many, er, *many*, wide-open available "politics *on* the table" tables. "Or," she goes on, "if neither is satisfactory, and you prefer to eat in one of the politically segregated dining rooms, though since they are already full at 7:00," she glances at her clipboard of reservations, ". . . and full

xiii

at 8:00 . . . and at 9:00 . . . and . . . well, you'd have to wait until, uh, midnight," she says sheepishly, "to get a seat."

Your dining room and table finally selected (though not entirely to your satisfaction), the cruise director continues.

"Which excursions do you plan to take? Snorkeling in a bleached, dead coral reef, an Arctic Ocean kayaking trip to see the one-half of the glaciers that remain, or an Amazon River trip to see the clear-cutting—or is what they're doing called 'clear-burning?'—of the rain forest?"

Startled, you stammer that these excursions aren't what you saw advertised in the brochures! She explains that due to the increasing acceleration of climate change, the cruise line's marketers can't print accurate brochures fast enough, and the ship apologizes for the inconvenience. To compensate, she goes on to say, "We've added a new excursion: a walk on top of the Great Pacific Garbage Patch, the largest floating island of plastic in the world, now estimated to be twice the size of Texas.[1] Won't it be remarkable," she asks, "to tell your grandchildren how much it's grown by the time they see it?" Depressed by the choices, you decline any excursion.

Your walk together into the grand foyer. You're startled to see in the center of this colossal, beautifully appointed space a cordoned-off, humble, but vintage VW Beetle. When you ask why it's there, the director, clearly pleased you asked the question, clips off a memorized speech:

> This 1971 VW Beetle is on display as a metaphor to show the amount of change the world has witnessed because of computing power. If that VW Beetle had undergone as many changes to its power and speed as has occurred to computer microchips, today that Beetle

would be able to go about three hundred thousand miles per hour. It would get two million miles per gallon of gas, and it would cost four cents! Intel engineers also estimated that if automobile fuel efficiency improved at the same rate as [microchips], you could, roughly speaking, drive a car your whole life on one tank of gasoline.[2]

You're speechless until you finally say that it's no wonder you've felt like the world is leaving you behind: because it is.

The director assures you that you haven't seen anything yet, and offers to take you on a tour. She points out people busy behind a wall of glass and explains it's the ship's newsroom; they pump out new stories 24/7 so you're never lacking for news of the ship. She leans in to whisper in your ear, "But you see the next room over, the one with the papered-over windows you can't see in? That's where the news bots are. They pump out fake news 24/7, too, and they're so good now you can't tell the difference from the real stuff. It's a problem for everyone on the ship. We've had riots because people believe the fake stuff, so watch your back, okay?" You whisper back your thanks.

You notice people standing idle in the ship's corridors; they don't seem happy like they're on vacation. The director explains that they used to be the ship's wait staff and chefs, but they've been replaced by more efficient robots. She mentions that you'll see more people who have been replaced by artificial intelligence, and others who know they will be. "They don't know what to do with themselves. It's sad, really," she concludes.

The tour goes on. She takes you to the top floor, which is under renovation for the top 1 percent of the wage earners who live on *The Mother Ship Earth*. Since they're accruing more and more wealth, they insisted they are entitled to expanded suites—dismissing the engineer's warnings that top-loading the ship will likely cause it to sink.

Together you descend belowdecks, where the tour also includes:

* A seminary classroom in which the professor is teaching the students how to earn a living wage in addition to serving a congregation, because fewer of them will earn one solely from parish ministry.

* A secret, Harry Potter–esque, cozy common room where preachers have gathered to talk about the tension in their congregations because of the divisive political climate. They say that parishioners are on the lookout for any hint of politics in their sermons. Some parishioners, they report, even accuse the preacher of ulterior motives when the Beatitudes are read in the scheduled course of the lectionary cycle. The complaint? The Beatitudes talk too much about the poor: that's politics! The preachers wring their hands; what can they do? They can't afford to make parishioners so mad it gets them fired; they have families to take care of—and seminary student loans to pay off. They need their jobs.

* Another room contains farmers lamenting the loss of their family farms that they sold to corporations out of financial desperation. They feel crushed to let down their pioneer ancestors who broke the ground on that land. Other farmers describe their helplessness to watch their nutrient-rich coastal topsoil give way to salt from rising sea levels. Coal miners and car factory workers join them; their jobs are disappearing too.

* A corporate board room contains Caucasian men seated around a large, oval table. These politicians and heads

of corporations, universities, and church denominations decry the encroachment of women and people of color into their ranks. How can they join forces to keep them out?

* One deck has live-in residents. The people on that deck look, worship, and talk like one another. When you arrive, they are in a meeting seeking consensus: what kind of lock would be secure enough for their floor's stairway doors, and what are the right tools to remove the elevator floor numbers, so that people from the lower decks can't rise up to take over the residents' deck in the dead of night?

* The ship is considering a move away from money altogether in favor of digital currencies, but they aren't sure yet. Digital currencies require so much energy to run, and the environmental studies are still pending.

* Already in the works, though, is the shift to driverless cars, trucks, and drones to deliver people and goods anywhere on the ship they need to go.

"Stop!" you cry. "I'm overwhelmed! Isn't there anything on this ship I would recognize? Anyplace that looks like home? It's too much!" you say. "Take me to a chapel! I need to pray!"

The director says she's happy to but wants to narrow it down to where you'll be happiest. Do you want a chapel for people who are spiritual but not religious; or one where LGBTQIA people can be ordained, married—or are banned; or a chapel where people say they welcome you but don't really, or don't care whether you're there or not as long as you pledge (and preferably, a lot)? In addition, she needs to know whether you would be okay with a big, cavernous, gorgeous nave with a few older people that's conveniently located to your berth, or would you prefer a thriving congregation that requires a hefty commute (but someday, in a driverless car, so the commute might be kind of fun)? "Oh, and the last thing," she says, "I need to know whether you're interested to actually help to build the reign of God right here, as you see it, on this *Mother Ship Earth*?"

The Sky *Is* Falling

The sky is falling! The sky is falling! Yes, in many ways it is. It really is. So let it. It's the only way we're going to get through this.

But how can we? Don't I see the consequences? Look what that falling sky is doing! There's too much at stake! We have to hold up the sky! If we let the sky fall, we'd have to say our good-byes to it, and we don't want to because it's the only sky we know. It's the sky we've woken up to every day of our lives. God painted that sky with these exact hues, with these particular brush strokes, with these shadings and nuances. It's the sky our parents and grandparents saw every morning of their lives. Granted, some of the colors are old and worn out and could definitely use some updating, but that's a lot of work, we have other things to do, and we all know what it's like to decide paint colors by committee. All in all, we'd just as soon not say good-bye to this sky, because it's the sky we know.

But we *can* let it fall. We *must* let it fall. We can let this sky fall because all that God made that falls, rises again. God is already painting a new sky, and we're all invited to grab a brush.

1

Letting the Sky Fall

There are people whose "skies fell," and they lived to tell the tale. Not many would say it was fun when they were getting pelted by the shards, but for all the trouble they endured, the new sky turned out okay. Here's an example.

This man was at the top of the food chain when his sky fell. His life was predictable; his sky was rigid, fixed, a brilliant sapphire blue of promise. He had identity and meaning, connections, status, education, a powerful, steady job—and minions to carry out his orders. Seven short words shattered his sky like a burst kaleidoscope: "Saul, Saul, why do you persecute me?"

After his sky fell, with no shard left above to soften the sun's brilliance, Saul was blinded by a light that accompanied the accusation. Led to Judas's house, he spent there three incomprehensible days. Paul must have felt as disoriented as if, still sightless, he were trying to grope for and fit the pieces of the kaleidoscope back together into its familiar patterns.

Saul/Paul gives us one of the most detailed records we have in Scripture of what can come undone when our skies fall.

Role[1]

Saul lost his function, the mantle that had been set on him. He had been trained as a Pharisee and understood himself to be a defender of the faith of his ancestors. Pharisees upheld the exact observance of Judaism, teaching of the law, and handing down of their customs and traditions.

Most of us experience the loss of familiar roles many times over. Two common roles that fall in a controlled manner are retirement and becoming "empty nesters." When we retire or our children leave home, we might not know what our role is anymore. Who are we now? What do we do with our time? What is our purpose when we no longer have to be a breadwinner or care for our kids?

A more sudden loss of role happens when our job industry falls apart or a child dies. Our role as provider may be at risk. The shock of no longer having a child at home sends parents reeling.

In a church with declining attendance, many clergy fear the loss of their roles not only as breadwinners, but as church leaders. As clergy, we've been raised up, set apart for our particular ministry. With the church in flux, many of us may not retain full-time positions. If we don't serve the church as clergy, who are we? What's our function? Will we be pseudo-laypeople sitting back in the pews?

Our roles are our functions, duties, and "place" within our communities. Our roles give us meaning. When we lose them we can also lose our sense of purpose.

The System

If Saul accepted that Jesus was, in fact, the Messiah, then the religious system Saul had learned, embraced, and taught, the one that created and maintained the rhythm of daily—even generational—life was up for grabs. What would he have left to stand on? What was true and real? What could he trust? Where would he place his loyalty?

We depend on systems daily, small and large. We depend on our system of traffic lights to function, and drivers to stop when they should. We depend on the health care system to provide competent medical care on demand. We depend on the church to proclaim the Word of God to each new generation, with each denomination and congregation creating its own systems to fulfill that mission. Americans depend on the system of checks and balances in our three branches of government, and our democratic system to choose our elected representatives.

Systems are born the first time they're used and quickly become entrenched. The downside to that entrenchment is they can't be moved by willpower—or common sense—alone. The upside is they provide a familiar framework we can, should, and need to count on. We need systems to get through each day. When sufficient forces collide, and the rigid systems we depend on are threatened, we can feel shaken from top to bottom.

Identity

The religious system that Saul was raised in provided him with his identity. He knew who he was, he knew his place in the world, and he could describe himself in relation to his religion. He formed an image of himself as he saw it reflected back by his tribe, the law, his outlook, and his purpose. He described his identity as "a member of the people of Israel, of the tribe of Benjamin, a Hebrew born of Hebrews; as to the law, a Pharisee; as to zeal, a persecutor of the church; as to righteousness under the law, blameless" (Phil 3:6). When Saul was confronted by the one he had so zealously been persecuting, all the identities by which he had defined himself were tossed out like so much chaff. He didn't know who he was. He needed those three days of silence in Judas's house to define a new identity.

When we say things like, "I don't recognize . . ." then finish the sentence with phrases such as *myself, this country, my church,* or *who you are anymore,* it's possible we're wrestling with our identity. When someone changes into something we don't recognize, it reflects back on us; we don't recognize ourselves in relationship to the change. This can also be reflected with expressions like, "This isn't the way I thought it would go"; "I don't know what to think, or what's real anymore"; or, "I'm not sure where my dreams (hopes, or expectations) went." We thought we could count on ourselves, the future, or the "rules," but when the sky falls, we might not know who we are in the broken pieces.

Livelihood

Saul lost his job. As an educated Pharisee, Saul had access to the work other Pharisees did, as a scribe or bureaucrat. I presume when Saul was chasing down Jesus-followers on behalf of the high priests, they gave him not only the letters of introduction he needed, but compensation for his troubles. However, if this voice he heard really was Jesus the Messiah, at the very least Saul would need extensive job retraining.

No means by which to earn a living lasts forever. Industries, local job markets, and even the church norm to call seminary-trained clergy and pay them a full-time stipend, come and go. Between ordinary fluctuations in job markets, the ways climate change will affect countless industries, and the increasing reliance on artificial intelligence, fewer of us can count on forty years of service with a gold watch waiting for us at the end. How will we pay the bills? How will we take care of our loved ones? What if we lose our health insurance and pension plans? What if we need extensive job retraining?

Lose your job, and it can feel like the sky not only falls, but hollows your stomach into that pit of fear.

Well-Being

We don't know about Saul's health prior to his conversion, but Paul suffered mightily for the cause of Jesus. He had that enigmatic "thorn in his flesh" (2 Cor 12:7–9), which remains a mystery. All we know is it was an affliction that tormented him enough that he begged Christ three times to relieve him of it. Request denied, by the way.

In addition, though Paul's literal death is not well documented, church tradition says at the end of his trial he was martyred by Nero. Regardless, given the beatings, hungry days, imprisonments, and floggings, there is no doubt of his willingness to give his entire well-being, that is, his life, to Christ.

Do I even need to say how it can feel like the sky of our well-being is falling when we hear the words, "You have cancer," or "Quit drinking, or you're going to die"? Or when we feel like stress, overwork, or worry might actually kill us?

Relationships

For Saul to trade his kinship loyalty from his blood family and tribe to Jesus, was a cultural no-no that's almost incomprehensible to our modern sensibilities. It was so severe a betrayal as to be beyond the pale. I can't help but wonder how Paul's parents, or his hometown synagogue and rabbi, cousins, and even his ancestors would have responded. Did they turn their backs to him? Rend their clothes? Pretend he never existed? And how did Paul himself feel after he turned to evangelizing the Gentiles only after his fellow Jews—the people to whom he was related and to whom he was closest—rejected his entreaties (Acts 13:5–7, 13, 44–48; 14:1–7; 17:1–2, 10; 18:5–6; 19:8–9)?

When we lose a friend, hero, coworker, spouse, lover, or child because of death, a breakup, relocation, or betrayal, it can shatter our worlds. But our worlds are not only broken apart by losing human relationships, but also pets, treasured heirlooms, photos, homes, beliefs, expectations, or faith.

Losing our faith is to lose our relationship with God. When that happens from shame, church betrayal, personal doubts, or unanswered questions, it can feel like we've truly entered Sheol.

What Next?

With thanks to Saul for showing us the pieces of the sky that can fall, when the pieces are strewn around our feet, how do we react? Well, it's often not pretty. We're in turmoil and all we want is to alleviate the pain. In our repeated attempts to do so, we often "do not do the very things we ought, and do the very things we ought not" (Rom 7:15). Scripture characters show how we can act irrationally, out of character, and hurt others in the process. We can see that many of them looked back, lashed out, or were enthralled by fear.

On the other hand, some did the very thing they ought: they lamented.

Look Back

Nostalgia is a pipe dream. We think we can go back to the past and gather those warm fuzzy memories like a Golden Retriever puppy and let him loose in the present. We believe with all our hearts he will remain a puppy, and never become the old, stubborn, and decrepit seventy-five-pound dog with bad hips who has to be carried outside into a Minnesota winter at 2:00 a.m. to relieve himself (not that I would know).

Some Scripture characters looked back, longing for the lives they left behind. The Israelites were freed from slavery, but the price they paid in hunger and thirst in an unforgiving desert was real. Manna took the edge off their hunger pangs, but the melons, cucumbers, and fresh water back in Egypt might be worth the tradeoff to return to slavery (Num 11:4–6). Fortunately the Israelites didn't succumb, but for other characters the lure of what they saw behind them was so strong they turned back, like the rich young man. When he heard the price he had to pay to follow Jesus—to sell all that he had and give it to the poor—it was just too high (Matt 19:21–22). He left Jesus on the spot to seek his old life.

There's truth in the phrase that comparison is the thief of joy, as Brené Brown says. When we compare "the good old days" to the present ones, the present ones may never measure up. After all, the old days are fixed in time with no competition, no new decisions to be made during them, and no other way they might have turned out. The present, however, is still sorting itself out, that is, whether it will become "good" old days, "bad" old days, or ordinary, forgettable days. When we compare present days to past days, we're not giving the present ones a fair chance to reveal their full character and complexity. Nostalgia is powerful indeed.

Lash Out

Externalize the pain and give the responsibility to fix it to someone else.

Just think how far back this behavior goes: all the way to the third and fourth human beings who ever existed, Cain and Abel. In a jealous rage over God's preference for his brother Abel's offering, and hoping to numb his emotional pain, Cain murdered Abel. It was not a successful strategy.

Centuries later, a disillusioned follower of Jesus named Judas also discovered lashing out didn't work. Judas felt Jesus had betrayed his disciples' faith and loyalty. To have been duped and betrayed was unforgivable. It was preferable to Judas to do damage control and betray the betrayer. That didn't turn out well for Judas.

Neither Cain nor Judas found lasting relief by lashing out, but only multiplied the grief for themselves and others. The same is true for us. Angry Twitter rants, shaming and bullying, whisper campaigns, intimidation, threats, and violence might feel pretty good in the moment, but they compound the pain. We take our hurt and behave selfishly and desperately, out of our normal minds, to offload it onto someone else.

Possessed by the Demon of Fear

Knowing the pain of their losses, but unsure whether the future would improve or only offer more of the same, many biblical characters who had divine encounters were so afraid of the consequences, that they responded out of fear. Take, for example, the disciples, the ones who said they were ready to "drink the cup" that Jesus drank, who pledged him their fealty, and were among the few who knew and declared Jesus to be the Messiah. Yet when the moment came to stand by him at his arrest and death, they fell apart, ran away, and hid. Panic overwhelmed them.

I know you know this, but I still need to put it in print: when we are scared, we don't act rationally. We're trying to survive and do whatever it takes. The more we feel painted into a corner, the more irrational we can become, and the worse the decisions we make.

We can be out of our minds with fear. We may not even know that's what we're feeling when we live with chronic fear in the forms of worry or anxiety. We can make a long string of really bad decisions that make so much sense—but only to us, and only at the time. We might choose bad investments, bad relationships, or the wrong job, overspend, overdrink, or accept bad advice.

When we're scared, we're not in our right minds because the demon of fear co-opts our frontal lobes.

Lament

Lament is not a bad thing, but a good, necessary, and fitting response. Lament causes us to turn inward; we look into ourselves to come to grips with our loss. We take long walks, pray, journal, and wrestle with our feelings. Looking inward for a time, we don't have the emotional bandwidth to look outward. We can't cope with others' problems, or even daily life for a spell. This is a normal, healthy response to loss.

Perhaps there was no greater example than Job. The entire book illuminates Job's lamentations and inner machinations as he struggled to come to grips with multiple, soul-crushing losses, and his confusion over why God would treat him so. Can anyone blame him?

The psalmists and prophets also lamented when they felt alone and isolated. "My God, my God, why have you forsaken me?" Psalm 22 weeps. Moses, Jeremiah, and other prophets had their moments of bitterness when the heaviness of the mantle of leadership buckled their knees, and they demanded of God, "Why me?" Why would God punish them by singling them out to lead such ungrateful, uncompromising people?

When we lose something or someone we value, we look and keep to ourselves for a while. We might also cry out in anguish, frustration, and anger over our own soul-crushing changes, releasing our sorrow while seeking some redemptive meaning.

When the sky falls, then, our minds and hearts are overwhelmed. To manage the pain we might look back, lash out, be gripped by the demon of fear, or most helpfully, lament. We lose our normal, recognizable minds as we try to come to grips with the scattered pieces of what used to be our normal, recognizable lives.

Letting the Sky Fall

Before I continue, I want to be clear about something important. Everything God created has a life span; literally nothing lasts forever. This vast universe is larger than our imaginations, but even it will one day cease. When that day comes, it might actually look like sky is falling. I'm just glad I won't be around to see it.

Between now and then, God does not cause our personal skies to fall. God no more causes skies to twist into tornadoes than God caused my three miscarriages. Skies fall. Change happens. Change is absolutely, completely, 100 percent unavoidable. That's why when the sky is falling and it's impossible to hold it up, we need to let it fall. When we don't let it fall, we're saying we don't trust God, that it's impossible for God to create a new sky. But more about trust in the next chapter.

What I'm about to say will seem to contradict what I just said, but stay with me. Sometimes the sky falls because God wills it, in that God calls us to lose one thing in favor of something else. God calls us to something new, as God called Saul, as God called many of us to an ordained or a lay preaching ministry. However, though God wills it and calls us, our compliance is optional. It is voluntary. We can say yes as much as we can say no. We are never forced. We can keep our sky as it is. For example, we can be called to the vocation of marriage, but accept or decline the invitation when our beloved proposes; we can be called to relocate when our beloved is called to a new job; we can be called to create justice and right old wrongs when we see harm wrought upon God's beloved, and say no—as we frequently do.

Other changes are not willed by God but thrust upon us out of the clear blue sky because we do not constitute our own universes. We are part of many things larger than ourselves, like relationships, systems, and the laws of creation God instituted from the beginning. When these change, they affect us. We do not choose or volunteer for the changes; we do not offer our consent for the changes to commence. Our compliance, or lack of it, is irrelevant. The change is upon us whether we like it or not, often irrevocably. The death of our beloved. The job that didn't materialize as promised after the relocation. Chronic, mental illness. The inside of a jail cell when demanding fair laws and dignity for others who have not received it. God does not cause these skies to fall.

Change is inevitable. However, a falling sky is not. That is, every falling sky comes with a change; not every change comes with a falling sky. Many changes are welcome ones. We may experience a change of role, identity, or well-being, and we know immediately the change is for the better. We're excited and embrace the change. We can feel breathless with gratitude and anticipation. The accompanying losses, like saying goodbye to friends when we relocate, quitting our job to head to seminary, giving up adult freedom to take on the responsibilities for our first baby, or accepting a new church call, have meaning. The price we pay in trade for these changes has purpose, and though the price may be costly, we're willing to pay it. We experience change, but the sky doesn't fall; indeed, it may look more intensely blue than ever, and the pieces fit together with barely a crack in the joints.

And there's the difference between whether the change feels like our sky is falling or not: it's the price we're willing to pay. If the price feels fair, or maybe even feels like we're getting a great deal, then the sky looks . . . cerulean—or is that a deep, ocean blue?

On the other hand, when the price we pay doesn't feel fair or have meaning—whether the change is physical, mental, geographic, symbolic, or monetary, and whether the currency is in roles, identities, relationships, well-being, systems, or livelihoods—it feels like our sky is falling, and we grieve. I'm not saying that's not normal, unreasonable, or human; it requires neither justification nor apology. When Jesus wept over the tomb of his friend Lazarus, he certainly never apologized for "falling apart," or not "being strong" or "holding it together." Of course not!

What I am saying is that change forces a choice: do I let this sky fall or not? If we try to hold up the sky, eventually it's going to fall anyway. When our beloved dies, we can strain with arms overhead trying to prevent that sky from falling until our knees buckle, but it won't matter. We'll lose that fight—every time.

Most often we finally exhaust ourselves from trying to hold up the pieces. We let them fall one by one, wherever they land, then gather them up and place most of them in the ground lovingly and for good. We hold back a few so we can recall with gratitude the particular shade of blue that reminds us of our beloved, use them for show and tell with others, and describe our beloved with more joy than longing. When we let the sky fall, a new sky is possible. When that happens, we're ready to accept a new beloved.

For preaching then, here's what this adds up to. The essence of a challenging sermon is not determined by the subject. *A challenging sermon is determined by the relationship the listener has to their sky.* It doesn't matter whether we're preaching that God's love means love oneself more, or love one's neighbors more justly; to accept God's forgiveness, forgive oneself, or forgive one's neighbors fully; to respect oneself as God's beloved, or respect one's neighbors as such. It doesn't matter if the sermon is perceived to be about gun control or gun rights, about welcoming immigrants or building more walls, about circling the wagons or opening the circle, or about loving sinners or hating sin. It doesn't matter whether a sermon speaks to environmental protection or job protection, a preferential option for the poor or a preferential option to work. It doesn't matter whether we preach none of the above, but something we say reminds listeners they're holding up a sky they're not yet ready to let go of. It also doesn't matter whether the form of the sermon is educational, pastoral, or prophetic. It's not the subject or its form that makes a sermon challenging for any one person; it's whether they're unwilling to let their arms fail and their sky fall.

From a practical point of view, then, if the sermon message comes at a time when listeners are finally ready to let their piece of sky fall, or they didn't realize they were holding it up and the price to drop it doesn't sound so bad, the listener feels comforted. They let that piece of sky fall. The preacher concludes the sermon, "Let the sky fall! God is painting another one, trust me!" The listener enthusiastically agrees. What a weight off their shoulders! The listener's response to the preacher? "Great sermon!"

Conversely, they may not be ready to let that piece go just yet. They're holding up their identity, belief, relationship, the good old days, or the system to which they have given their loyalty, and it would feel too humiliating to do an about-face. When the preacher concludes the sermon, "Let the sky fall! God is painting another one, trust me!," well, that price is too high. The response? "How dare you preach that sermon!"

That brings us to the gospel we don't want to hear: we have to lose our life in order to gain it. "For those who want to save their life will lose it, and those who lose their life for my sake, and for the sake of the gospel, will save it" (Mark 8:35). Let's be clear, though: in losing our life to gain it, Jesus isn't giving us an if-then conditional statement. Jesus isn't saying *if* you lose your life, you will prove yourself to me; I will enjoy watching you ache and mourn, and when you have cried enough, *then* you will gain the gospel. No!

Jesus is *describing* what happens. When we try to save our old life by holding up the sky though it is crumbling around our ears, we are *losing* our life. When we insist our skies cannot fall because we can't live without them, we are declaring only death is real, and resurrection is not. While we are thus wasting our breaths, we are losing out on the abundant life available to us. We're so busy catching falling pieces and trying to glue them back up, we can't see another sky has been started. The primer and paint color swatches have already been applied, ready for us to select.

However, when we do let those pieces fall, and trust God that together we can paint a new one, we are *gaining* our life. The color won't be the same shade of blue as before, but we can see that lapis or aquamarine—or even a more subdued shade like denim that holds some gray—is allowing possibility and hope to lay claim on us again. We can consent to God's will and call to be resurrected: to live, love, and serve again. That's what it looks like when our life is saved. We love again, love newly, love differently. This is the gospel we need to hear.

Questions for Reflection

These questions for reflection are intended for personal meditation or for use with preaching colleagues. They are intended to help you step back and think about the preaching experience and your own personal responses to the topic and the task.

1. What's a change you've experienced that didn't feel like the sky was falling? What were the circumstances? Consider your role, systems, identity, well-being, livelihood, and relationships. What were the consequences of the change to any or all of these? During the change, how did you respond? Did you look back or lash out? Were you possessed by the demon of fear? Did you lament? Tell this story in words, pictures, song, dance, or sculpture.

2. What's a change you've experienced when it felt like the sky did fall? What were the circumstances? Consider your role, systems, identity, well-being, livelihood, and relationships. What were the consequences of the change

to any or all of these? During the change, how did you respond? Did you look back or lash out? Were you possessed by the demon of fear? Did you lament? Tell this story in words, pictures, song, dance, or sculpture.

3. Describe another time when you held up your sky. How did it affect losing or gaining your life for the sake of the gospel?

4. Describe another time when you let your sky fall. How did it affect losing or gaining your life for the sake of the gospel?

5. Think of two sermons when parishioners reacted favorably to your message. Imagine their skies. Imagine the color. Imagine how the sermon might have sounded to them with regard to their roles, systems, identity, well-being, livelihood, and relationships. Which of these might have felt reinforced by the sermon?

6. Think of two sermons when parishioners reacted against the message. Imagine their skies. Imagine the color. Imagine how the sermon might have sounded to them with regard to their roles, systems, identity, well-being, livelihood, and relationships. How did they react against the message? Did they look back or lash out? Were they possessed by the demon of fear? Did they lament?

7. After considering your experiences and those of your listeners, how does this affect your relationship toward them? Would you preach those sermons differently or not? Why?

What You Need to Know

* The parts of the sky that fall include our identity, roles, systems, livelihoods, well-being, and relationships.
* Attempting to assuage our pain, we might look back, lash out, be possessed by the demon of fear, and/or lament.
* The essence of a challenging sermon is not the sermon's subject or form but the relationships listeners have to their skies.

2

Building Mutual Trust

Jesus tells us to trust him all the time. Often not in so many words, but he says it just the same. It's no wonder, because trust is everything.

For example, Jesus often says, "Do not be afraid." It's implied we can trust what he's saying, as in, "Do not be afraid; trust me." Or an expanded version might be, "Do not be afraid. I know the sky is falling, and right now you have every reason to be afraid. Just the same, be still, do not be anxious, and trust me; I know what I'm talking about. I've seen something your eyes aren't open to yet. I've heard something you don't have ears to hear yet. You're focused on what's scary, but I know there's more to the story. If I told you what's possible after this, you wouldn't believe me, and you won't believe me until you discover it your-self. Between now and then, listen to my voice. Trust me."

If we give Jesus the benefit of the doubt for a moment, what is it, exactly, we're asked to trust? Well, I don't think we're asked to trust that Jesus will patch the cracks in our skies and make them stay intact and in place. That would mean nothing ever changes and no one ever dies, so that can't be what he meant.

It also can't mean to trust that when the sky falls, those tumbling shards won't hurt when they pierce us. Jesus was "deeply moved" and wept at his friend Lazarus's tomb, and over Jerusalem's intransigence. When Jesus was hanging on the cross, he wondered where God had gone. Really? Jesus was worried God might have something more important on the calendar than hanging with his son while he died? Wherever God went for those three hours, Jesus felt hurt. That falling skies won't make us cry out in pain doesn't seem to be what Jesus meant either.

It also doesn't look like we're supposed to trust that when the sky is about to fall we don't feel actual fear. In the Garden of Gethsemane the night before he was crucified, Jesus was "grieved and agitated" (Matt 26:39), and asked God three times whether the cup could pass from him. That sounds to me like he was afraid, and it was a perfectly normal fight-or-flight human response. I don't think Jesus meant we could trust him to shut down our protective sympathetic nervous system, which God designed in God's "very good" human creation to warn us of danger and keeps us alive. For Jesus to feel the human response to "be afraid and flee" from his own crucifixion demonstrates we weren't created with a design flaw. Not to feel the physical sensations of fear also can't be what Jesus meant.

If it's none of those things then, when Jesus says, "Even though your sky is falling, do not be afraid; trust me," what is he suggesting? He's suggesting we trust in hope, faith, and love—and the greatest of these is love.

Hope

Hope means we trust that what's in front of us isn't all there is. Hope means we trust in a future we cannot see, or only see through a glass darkly. There is something better, something good, or at least something salvageable, that will emerge from the current situation. To hope is to dream, to imagine, to dare that something good is around the next bend; we're moving toward it and believe it's waiting to greet us. To hope is to extend ourselves outward, beyond ourselves. When our skies are falling and we don't have hope, we believe this is truly the end of all things. We look to the ground and let those pieces drive us into it and crush us. We don't bother to search for the new sky already under construction. Hope, on the other hand, keeps our gaze stubbornly fixed on the eastern horizon, looking for that first light that changes the shade ever so slightly from midnight blue to navy.

No matter where our hope is placed, it's risky. We place something we value in someone else's hands, and hope they honor and respect it. We place our dreams, desires, prayers, and needs in God's hands. We place the needs of the community in the hands of politicians. We place our health care needs in the hands of doctors, nurses, and medical insurance executives. We place our home values in the hands of homeowner associations, the Federal Reserve, and financial industries. We place our money in banks, our children in schools, and the Christian formation of teens with youth leaders. We place our expectations in ministers, preachers, and bishops. We place our hearts in the hands of spouses, lovers, friends, and pets; in memories, homes, and columbariums. Hope places our trust in another, and we know not what future they may bring. Hope risks; so therefore does trust.

Hope is not only risky, it's dangerous to those who would steal our hope away. Hope never settles for the "now" but trusts in the "not yet." Hope refuses to look into the eyes of oppression, but peeks over its shoulder to see liberation sneaking up from behind. Hope is a threat to all who are determined to make us believe now is as good as it gets.

When the sky is falling, we do not have to be afraid when we trust in the hope there is abundant life ahead.

Faith

What does it mean to have faith when Jesus tells us not to be afraid? Specifically, Jesus asks us to trust he'll get the job done because he's dependable, reliable, and capable. That said, and with all due respect to our Lord and Savior, our experience is often different. There is too much evidence to list that Jesus appears undependable, unreliable, and incapable. Enough so that many—myself included—want to retort, "Show me the money." Where's the disconnect?

First, let's remember Jesus isn't our personal virtual assistant waiting on our command. When our car hits black ice and we go airborne, we might yell to Siri, "Call Jesus: mobile!" And when Jesus picks up, we're likely to bellow to suspend the car right-side up three inches off the ground and set us down gently. As genuinely sympathetic as Jesus will be, we'll probably still crash. Jesus helped design the laws of physics, like gravity, that bring us back down to earth with velocity (a lot of it), mass (a lot of that, too), and time (not nearly enough of this one). Hence our predicament in an airborne car. Those natural laws that are generally good for us still apply when we don't want them to.

Likewise, *E. Coli* bacteria in our colons are necessary for human life. But outside their divinely prescribed arena they do humans great harm, even though the bacteria are still functioning exactly as they are supposed to according to their God-given natures. God does not change their properties when they escape our guts to go forth and multiply in minor flesh wounds.

God also didn't stop fifty-one inches of rain from falling during a hurricane on the Houston metro. That colossal amount of rain is due in no small part to humans' warming of ocean waters. Dump that amount of water where six million people live on a coastal plain (including yours truly) without sufficient water drainage built into the infrastructure, and not even Jesus can bail water fast enough to make a difference. That disaster's on us. No, the laws of nature and the consequences of human actions apply equally to the righteous and the unrighteous.

So no, Jesus doesn't obey our commands like the perfect virtual assistant, but that's not enough to lose faith in his competence.

About Miracles

But what about miracles? Aren't those in Jesus's job description? That's a longer subject for another day, so I'll just say this. I believe there are miracles, but if a miracle means God temporarily alters the laws of nature to our preferences, I'm skeptical that many of the miracles we say are miracles are actually so. Here's why. My first career was surgical intensive care nursing in a hospital serving a five-state region. It was a Trauma One center, and we got in all the "train wrecks." I saw some people make it after horrific accidents when I wouldn't have bet a nickel they would have. Were their recoveries miraculous? Maybe. There's no way to know for sure. What bothers me is at what point in the process do we claim the miracle? After a patient has spent seven months in the ICU, bankrupting them and their families in the process? They will owe the hospital hundreds of thousands of dollars for the implementation of their miracle, only to face a lifetime of chronic consequences—and further expense—from their injuries.

Plus, ascribing miracles begs the question how God decides on whom and when to bestow them. For instance, was a miracle bestowed on the man who was airlifted to my hospital, whose razor-slit wrists I bandaged after he tried to kill himself—and whose ankles were cuffed to the bedrail? Perhaps. But a miracle would have been timely for his wife and three children whom he had murdered a few hours before. No, I'm not persuaded if we pray fervently enough, or enough times, or in exactly the right way, or just because of the mood Jesus is in that day, Jesus will suspend the laws of nature long enough to give some a window of escape from catastrophe, but not others.

But what do I know? Pray for miracles; maybe that's exactly what God is doing. But for me, the miracle is God's relentless, intransigent faithfulness, care, curiosity, and compassion that imbues the human spirit and drives us to help others in need—even when we're the ones who cause the problems in the first place that cause people to be in need. The miracle to me is God doesn't give up on us. When we consent to God's compassion we are driven to solve problems for others through research, experimentation, and financial donations, and through systems like health care. Indeed, it will be a true miracle when we as a nation agree to pay for excellent health care delivery for the poor, and the chronically and mentally ill. That miracle would come from God's concern for us, which in turn inspires us to do what we can for each other. God's stubborn grace is totally in Jesus's job description; see below.

If we are to trust that Jesus is reliable, dependable, capable, and on the job as God's only begotten, Jesus learned from the best. He is fully able to perform his duties and hasn't missed a single day of work. He and God collaborated to write his job description, and we humans were not invited to tweak it. His job description is to dwell in us so we are one with God. Moreover, since Jesus is still living and contains the wisdom of the Spirit, in consultation with his fellow members of the Trinity, it is within Jesus's scope of practice to interpret and implement his job for each generation.

Because Jesus dwells in us, we cannot be separated from God while our skies are falling. In our generation, we are not separated from God because of opioid addiction, or because of those who prescribed the pills. We are not separated while we are reaping the consequences of our greed and folly that pollutes the earth that is the source of our life and well-being. We are not separated because advances in technology outpace our development of the ethics to employ them, or to keep that technology safe from hackers, malware, and bots.

We may deny ourselves God's love, care, and forgiveness, but that doesn't mean Jesus separates himself from us. If he did, it would get him written up for neglecting his duties and negate the whole point of the resurrection. He still forgives us the sins of our day, of our generation's own making. Jesus still dwells in us and we in the Holy Trinity, even if we don't change course. If it comes to it, Jesus will go down with the good *Mother Ship Earth* even though we're the ones who stood inside the engine room and blew up a hole in the starboard side. Even then. Even with us. Even now.

Because Jesus dwells in us, we have the capacity to see our mistakes, and address and apologize for them; see the suffering of others and meet them; and see the needs of today's poor, widows, orphans, migrants, strangers, and foreigners among us, and tend to them. Dwelling in us is Jesus's job description for which he is uniquely qualified, competent, and utterly reliable.

Neither God nor the Spirit complain about Jesus's work performance. It is only we who accuse him of dereliction of duty. Trust him. He's on the job.

Love

When we trust Jesus loves us, we trust he sees us as we are, where we are, and the condition we are in. Because he sees us, he wants the best for us. Wanting the best for us means Jesus wants the dignity of every human being not only to be respected, but enabled to thrive. Jesus means he not only wants justice for every human being, and especially the poor, but expects us to provide it and holds us accountable when we don't. When Jesus says we can trust he is truly present in the breaking of bread and the gathered community, that makes us one however much we may disagree with one another. When we trust Jesus, we know the foundational truth of our belonging and worth is in our being created and seen as "very good." When we trust we are loved, even when the sky is falling down around our ears, we trust Jesus sees us as his mother saw him in his agony on the cross, and had the courage to stay to the end. Because he sees us, our hurts are felt in his flesh. Our cries sear his heart. Our suffering twists his gut.

What good does all that empathy and compassion do for us, though, if Jesus is counting the hairs on our head when they're fifteen feet under the rubble? What makes Jesus's love worth trusting in? To what end? To answer that question, let's first consider what happens when we don't feel seen.

If we suffer a loss and feel its grief but don't have our loss acknowledged, we don't feel seen. It can drive us inward and distance us from others; we don't trust if we talk about how we really feel, we won't be laughed at and isolated. With sincere respect to any reader who might identify as a "cat lady," allow me to illustrate. If a cat lady has seventeen cats in her small apartment and cat fourteen dies, many would struggle to find respect for her grief. Rather than empathize, many would feel creeped out by the idea of living with seventeen cats, feel relief for the cat who had escaped, and roll their eyes upward as her eyes pour out her sorrow. If she seeks consolation by talking about cat fourteen, what's she likely to hear? "Don't worry about it! You have sixteen more!" Her response might be to lash out in anger, or perhaps more likely, to withdraw into the company of her remaining cats, as they are the only ones who understand and share her grief. Feeling shamed and alone, she is less likely to trust others will grieve with her when her other cats cross the rainbow bridge. If she is to trust she is loved, she has to be able to trust that her unique grief and her relationship to cat fourteen, known to her alone, is honored. She counted every hair on cat fourteen; who is counting hers? Who dignifies her experience that she is human with a heart that breaks?

This is why it matters even when we're fifteen feet under the broken rubble of our skies, that we trust we're loved: it dignifies our humanity. Though the world is falling apart with our little corner of it in shambles, it still matters to God because it matters to us. Love shows we are unique in our experience of the world, which uniquely reveals the image of God to the rest of it. And that matters. Love helps us understand we may feel alone but are never sent away from the banquet table. Trusting in love may not glue the pieces of the sky back together or rescue us from difficulty, but it says, "I see. I'll stay by your side." What else in the universe can promise as much?

And why is the greatest of these three—hope, faith, and love—love? Hope has a shelf life. Eventually we learn whether what we hope for has come to pass. Justice for the poor happens, or it doesn't. Our bodies are healed, or they're not. The family leaves politics off the menu for Thanksgiving dinner, or it doesn't. Even if we don't find out until the next life, eventually all things are revealed. (Or I hope they are anyway.) If hopes are dashed, we create new hopes, but those new hopes will also someday be fulfilled or not, and we start over. Likewise, faith ends because it has an expiration date: the day of our deaths. After we die, we will no longer look through that glass darkly but see God face to face. We won't need faith anymore. Its utility will have passed because we'll know. (Or I have faith this is so, anyway.)

But love? Love never ends. Love has no shelf life, no expiration date. It has no birth date with a first inhalation and cry to declare it is alive, and no final death rattle when it breathes its last. It's the one thing that existed before the Big Bang, and it will exist long after this universe has been drawn in by the force of its own gravity and contracted to something smaller than a pinhead. Love is infinite and timeless, and it functions by its own laws—always to grow, never to cease, forever to expand, while always drawing us in. Because love never ends, within this holy Trinity of trust, love is the greatest of these three.

Building Trust

Trust between preacher and listener is literally essential if the listener is to believe letting go of their falling skies is going to be OK. In fact, we can intentionally build hope, faith, and love between preacher and listener. In Dickens's *A Christmas Carol*, Mr. Scrooge places his hand in the hands of each of three spirits to guide him to places he dreaded. They visited painful memories and regrets from his past, discovered just how contemptibly he was viewed by his own family (whom he secretly loved) in the present, and saw the loneliness and isolation this would bring him in the future. Why did Mr. Scrooge go willingly? Trust. With fear and trembling, to be sure, but still he gave the spirits his trust.

If listeners are going to place their trust in us to go places they don't want to go, we need to make a concerted effort to build that trust. It's too critical to leave it to happenstance. How can we be intentional about laying the foundation and building trust, layer by layer? There are three necessary overlapping practices that build trust in the center. We *diagnose* how much trust we have built and can risk expending, *experiment* to build more, and *appraise* our efforts to see whether trust is accumulating.

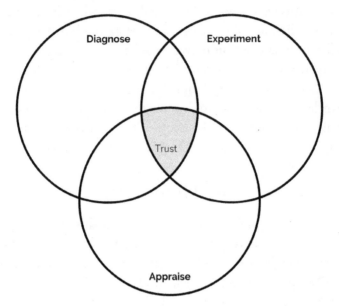

Diagnose

Most of us have a sense we can't preach a deliberately and overtly provocative sermon every Sunday, and it takes time to develop enough trust with a congregation to preach that first challenging message. We often rely on intuition to decide when, what form, how often, and to what degree we can preach a deliberately challenging sermon. However, intuition is good—but it isn't foolproof. Sometimes we get it wrong, and the consequences can be devastating. It's more reliable if intuition has backup. After all, intuition isn't formed *ex nihilo*, but from experience interpreted with the help of the Spirit in nanoseconds. Intuition is formed so quickly we don't recognize the experience or the senses that formed it. Looking at samples of behaviors will help us better diagnose whether our intuition is correct before preaching a difficult message.

A first step to build trust is to discern how much of each of the three aspects of trust we have to work with. How do we decide? First, we start with ourselves.

Consider each of the three aspects of trust: hope, faith, and love. How trustworthy are you? Do you place your hope in, and risk (appropriately), what you value with those you serve? For example, do you express your hope in the future of the church, your congregation, and the creativity of humanity to solve its problems? Is your affect hopeful, or crabby, anxious, or pessimistic? What do your facial expressions and body language say about the hope you place in God and in them? Do you place your hopes more in God's capacities, or in your own to bring about the reign of God?

How faithfully reliable, dependable, and competent are you? Can people count on you? If it's a parish value, do you show up on time and prepared? Can listeners trust you have taken into account their own cultural norms and experiences, and how these affect their participation in the life of the congregation? Do you show up at bedsides, mortuaries, and prison cells? Are you competent? Do you know what you're doing? If not, do you ask for help and have the humility to learn, seek feedback, and apply it? Do you show faith in your parishioners by asking them to teach you, whether it's parish finances, knitting, or golf?

How much do you love them? Are you sincere; do you mean what you say and say what you mean? Do you keep confidences because you said you would? Do you see them as a child of God, and respect them as God's child (even if you disagree)? Do you ask them questions about their lives, and take their experiences to heart, without arguing that their experiences were wrong? Do you empathize, offer pastoral care, and do your best to see life from their point of view? Do you let them know you care about them?

I suggest doing a quick circle sketch (or if you're more ana-lytical, create a spreadsheet and score yourself from one to ten). With a pencil or erasable pen, shade each circle below. (We'll come back to this, so use something you can erase with.) The darker the circle, the more trustworthy you believe yourself to be.

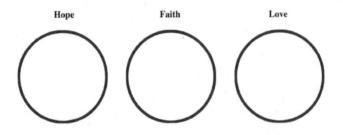

In addition to what has made you trustworthy, you also have to consider what may have lost you trust. Have you showed you really don't have hope for the future of the parish by publicly lamenting the parish doesn't give enough in pledges to keep you employed full time? Have you been unwilling to ask for help and learn from parishioners? Have you demonstrated you're unreli-able, undependable, or incompetent? Have you looked past or through people in their hurts, beliefs, perspectives, or opinions that differ from your own? Have you expressed macro- or micro-aggressions with regard to race, sexual orientation, or political affiliation? Have you outright hurt people that would cause them to think again before they trusted you in the future?

Consider the trust you may have lost. In each of the circles above, erase to bring it to the shade you think you've earned. (If you're using a spreadsheet, subtract from your subtotals.)

Perception

In what areas do you believe you are not only trustworthy, but demonstrably so? That is, you may know yourself to be trustworthy, but what behaviors and "vibes" would others witness and attest to so they have evidence that putting their trust in you is wise?

This is the sticky wicket. You may know yourself to be trustworthy. Your circles above may be black with trust! You know people could trust you completely, and believe the behaviors you exhibit match and deepen the trust people can place in you.

However, when it comes to people placing their trust in you, the only thing that matters is their *perception*. It is of utmost importance. On the one hand, there is nothing we can do about people's perceptions of us. People form them, hold onto them, are reluctant to talk to us about them, and undoing them is much harder than creating them in the first place. Perceptions are formed about both our trustworthiness and untrustworthiness. Some will trust us because we wear a collar around our necks, and others will distrust us for the same reason and in greater measure. For others, no matter what we do or the evidence we supply to the contrary, they are entrenched in their opinion.

The latter can happen for example, when parishioners distrust the church authorities who closed their beloved church building no matter how scarlet red the parish balance sheet was. It is equally true that people can place more trust in clergy than is deserved. They might trust clergy implicitly simply because of the office we hold. They can hang on to this opinion no matter the evidence. This is seen, for example, after a clergy person is convicted of embezzlement or sexual impropriety, and yet some people's trust will remain unflappable. There is nothing we can do to adjust people's perceptions; that's one of the hazards of leadership.

Just the same, it's our responsibility to do everything in our power to make ourselves as worthy of others' trust as possible. This relies on the same principle that preachers cannot control the message a listener hears from our sermons, and yet it is no less incumbent upon us to continue to improve our communication skills so we are as clear as our abilities allow. That is a preacher's job, and the extent of our responsibility. What we say is our responsibility; what is heard is not. Likewise, it is also our job, our responsibility, to do everything in our control to be as worthy of people's trust as we can be.

Listeners will not follow us through the desert of letting our old selves go in order to be reborn in Christ if they don't perceive we hope for God's best for them, that we're faithful in living out our call, and we love them by holding their best interests at heart. Think about this: if someone told you you're going to die, and that it's going to be painful and disorienting, but worth it— "trust me"—what would it take for you to follow them?

As a result, we also need to diagnose as best we can how people perceive our trustworthiness in each of the three aspects of hope, faith, and love. For the next week, imagine someone is filming you. What would the movie reveal? What cues would people pick up that get mixed into their intuition about how much they can trust you? Would they add evidence to a consistent pattern of being unprepared, or breezing in and out of a hospital room in too much of a hurry to sit for a spell? Would they add evidence to trusting that you mean what you say when you say no, you're not available to meet because you have that time set aside for sermon prep, seeing your spiritual director, or vacation? Would they add evidence you see and love them when you listen without defensiveness to painful disclosures of your racism that shows up subtly in your sermons?

It doesn't matter how trustworthy we see ourselves; to build trust, it only matters what someone perceives. Return to the circles above, and add and subtract pencil or ink based on how you think your trustworthiness is perceived (or add or subtract from each subtotal).

Experiment

For the perception of trust to be built, our actions have to be visible. Our gestures have to be witnessed. We are rewarded by our Father in heaven who sees us pray—or perform good and trustworthy acts—in secret, and that is all well and genuinely good. But building trust requires the right hand to know what the left hand is doing. For example, it's a holy act to visit those in prison once a month, but if the only thing parish leaders know is you're not in the office every third Thursday between two and five, that creates an information vacuum. Trust is built on information interpreted to form someone's perception of our trustworthiness. To build trust means we intentionally offer the information needed that demonstrates our trustworthiness. What kinds of information might that be?

The following are sweeping categories to consider, not specific suggestions. You know yourself, your situation, and the people involved. You will recognize some suggestions as too high a risk in your context, or they might feel manipulative rather than authentic. I trust you to apply the ideas to yourself and your people in your unique situation. I'm suggesting what you can do, not what you should.

Hope. Risk what you value and make it vulnerable to your parishioners.

* Share your hopes and dreams for your ministry, your congregation, the church, and/or your personal interests.
* Share your quirks and passions, not to the point of boring people, but so they know what brings you joy—because joy in itself is vulnerable.
* Dream big in parish meetings about the future of your congregation, neighborhood, and world. Work backward. What would it take to make the dream a reality?
* Let others make decisions that influence yours.
* Let others take on a task and run with it, even if it isn't completed to your standards.
* Give the best preacher on your staff access to the pulpit, no matter their official position or job description; risk the gospel being spread well.

Faithful. Be vulnerable, reliable, dependable, and competent. Get curious.

* Ask parishioners what they do (regarding career, home life, or interests) and how they do it. For instance, ask a busy mom who manages home and work life in addition to attending church, how she does it.
* Try something new, and be willing to fumble publicly; take voice lessons from your choir director and risk singing a solo; ask the parish treasurer to teach you the accounting software the parish uses, even if she'll see you struggle with math; or ask the parish's master gardener the best way to grow roses, even if yours never bloom as well.
* Tell your parish leaders you've asked your bishop for a mentor, that you see a spiritual director or therapist, or

you're taking an online course to become a more effective preacher.

* Show up as agreed, and be prepared.
* Inform people when things change and why.
* Keep confidences.
* Take your "stuff" to your therapist and spiritual director so your people can count on you to be fully present to them.
* Go the "mile" you agreed to, but not the extra one if you want to model what "enough" looks like.
* Go out for coffee with those you know hold opposite theological, political, or social views for the sole purpose of asking them to educate you about their point of view. Hard as it may be to want to argue, stick to your promise to be educated to demonstrate that they can rely on your word.
* To be clear is to be kind: what can you do, what are you willing to do, how will the task get done, and when will it be completed? Breaches of trust occur routinely over fuzzy expectations for tasks.
* Thank staff members publicly, especially when they do a job better than you would have.
* To build competence into the picture, what level of quality does a project need to have? What will be included, and what's left out? When is it due, and to whom?
* Do you have the expertise and experience required for a project?
* Do you have the time, energy, bandwidth, and resources needed?

✳ Are you willing, and will this bring you joy?
✳ Will it build the reign of God?

To be a faithful preacher, we demonstrate our reliability and competence through the ways we prepare.

✳ Have you done your homework about Scripture, current events, the lives of those you serve, and the needs of the neighborhood?
✳ Have you allowed the Scriptures to affect you so that you believe the good news you preach?
✳ Do you share the faith you have, and the faith you don't, by sharing doubts and questions?
✳ Do you preach ethically by preaching what you believe is true? Or do you preach what you think you "should" preach, or what you think people want to hear? Do you water down your messages so as not to rock any boats?
✳ If you're not very skilled and have trouble offering a coherent message that keeps listeners' attention—if you are consistently demonstrating a lack of competence—are you willing to get help?

Love. For listeners to trust us, they have to feel seen, heard, and valued. I know you know that listening and pastoral care are paramount. Pastoral care builds the relationship like nothing else, and is essential to implementing any change (which we'll talk more about in the next chapter). Unlike the suggestions above that are more wide-ranging, here I will narrow the topic of seeing to preaching. Specifically, if we're asking people to trust us that dying to self is worth it, we need to let them know we see what dying might cost them.

Change affects people, and asking people to change means asking them to let something go to make way for something new. We need to see, if only in our imaginations, which people are affected, by how much, and what they might value that is being put at risk. The people in your congregation may or may not be the ones directly affected, but they are connected to others they know, love, and care for.[1] As a member of the interconnected communion of saints, we need to be aware that what feels like a benign suggestion to us might step on not only the toes of the saints who are present in the nave, but those who are not. If we don't "see" the saints, *all* of them, it can greatly jeopardize the relationship and erode trust.

I suggest making maps or spreadsheets, or writing narratives, as you prefer, that you can add to and adjust over time. The purpose is to guesstimate the price your sermon message is asking listeners to pay, with the added "tax" of their trust that you might also have to pay. A radial map can be especially helpful to visualize the ripple effects. For example, if you plan to suggest a specific change in your sermon, write that change in the center surrounded by the six areas identified in chapter 1: systems, well-being, livelihood, identity, role, and relationships.

Let's say you preach a sermon about Psalm 104 that praises God's creation and care for the Earth. You suggest one way we can treat the Earth with the care God does, is to decrease greenhouse gasses by cutting down on methane emissions produced by cow manure, and by eating less beef and more plants. To eat less beef and more plants seems (at least to me) to be a benign, small-scale experiment in love for our neighbor and the earth. Consider this, though: who might be affected by this suggestion?

To imagine who might be affected, let's expand just one of the six areas: livelihood. Livelihood is a broad category that includes every which way people are able to care for their short- and long-term needs, including holding a job, pensions, health care, retirement, investments, and the resources to start over in a different profession if necessary.

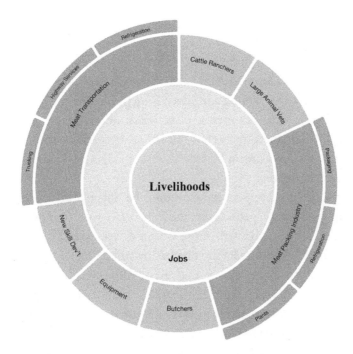

Continuing down one of those rabbit trails, let's expand on jobs. Whose jobs might be affected if people ate less meat to positively affect the environment? The point is not to be exhaustive but to see the communion of saints who aren't necessarily in the room when we preach. I thought of cattle ranchers, local butchers/grocers, slaughterhouses, the large animal veterinary industry, the meatpacking industry, and the meat transportation industry. Focus on just two of those, and we find more people who could be affected. Expanding on the meatpacking industry, there are packing supplies, refrigeration, and meatpacking plants. For meat transportation, there are truckers, refrigerated trucks, and the service-related industry for truckers. How also might people of color, the marginalized, and underrepresented populations be affected?

We could continue on each of the groups represented and the supporting industries for each of those groups. For example, I didn't get to marketing and advertising industries, the financial industry that loans money to all of those industries, or national and global financial markets—nor the congregations who might be affected downstream by a decrease in pledges or their endowment investments.

None of these people who could be affected are necessarily in your congregation, but they are related to, friends with, or friends of friends with those who are. We can't take anyone for granted. We can't let anyone be invisible. Out of sight can't mean out of mind because they aren't off God's mind. I'll get into preaching specifics in later chapters, but for now suffice it to say, to build trust requires us first to see our neighbors and have all their best interests at heart; and second, to preach out loud that we see our suggestion might affect some adversely. They need to know we know the suggestion might come with pain and sacrifice.

See the whole map to this point in my brainstorming (p. 44), and it's easy to visualize the rings of people whose livelihoods could be affected by one small suggestion. My point is not that a sermon has to solve all problems, or that we back off from the gospel. My point is that to build trust, people and those they love need to feel seen and that they matter. To render people invisible, and their needs and values inconsequential, erodes trust and is antithetical to the great commandment to love our neighbors as ourselves. Mapping, making lists, outlines, or drawing stick figures makes us aware of the consequences and the price we could be asking people to pay on behalf of the gospel. It's not that we shouldn't pay the price, but if listeners don't believe the preacher and God have their best interests at heart, and the price goes unacknowledged, why would they pay it? Why would any of us?

Appraise

With each small experiment, it's important to appraise the outcome. To appraise means to find the value in something (rather than what's wrong with it) so we know what to capitalize on the next time. This is the essence of intentional practice: decide what to try next; try it; stop; notice what worked; decide what to do next; and so on.

For each action, notice what you did and what happened directly afterward. What did you see and hear? Does what you see and hear correlate with increasing or decreasing trust? How can you check that assumption? On the basis of what worked, what would you repeat? What would you adjust? What will you try next? How will you extend hope? How will you be faithful? How will you love more?

Make a Plan

Based on the suggestions above or ideas of your own, make a plan. How will you deepen hope, faith, and love in ways your people can see? Choose two items for each one you'll work on over the next three months.

Keep a journal of the things you notice in the congregation. When there's tension and separation, or harmony and closeness, diagnose what's happening with trust: where is hope growing or lacking? In what ways are people being faithful, or not on task or mission? Where do people see one another? When do they tell

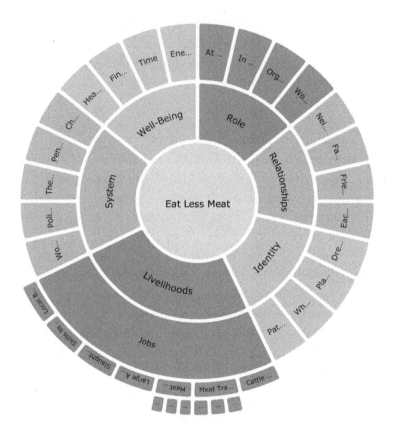

Role: church; organizations; work; in the family

Relationships: self; neighbors; family; friends

Identity: dreams/hopes; plans/expectations; who I understand myself to be; patterns that work to my benefit

Livelihoods: butchers; cattle ranchers; meat transportation (trucking, highway services, refrigeration); new skills for new career; meat packing (plants, packing, refrigeration); large animal vets; skill development to start over with a new career

System: theology; church; work; political party; pension

Well-Being: health; finances; energy/bandwidth; time

faith stories, describe their experiences, and deeply listen? When are people dismissing each other?

Also journal what's happening theologically. In what ways do you and your listeners indicate they trust or distrust God? Diagnose whether it's about hope, faith, or love. What dots got connected that led to that conclusion? What might this suggest about the theology you preach for a period of time?

Yes, I know this takes time, and who has more of that? But given where we're headed together, and that trust is everything, there's no more important use of it.

Conclusion

There's a reason we aren't yet living the reign of God: we haven't built it yet. We know we're supposed to build it, and we know God has equipped us with the resources and grace to accomplish it. Yet why haven't we? In short, we don't trust God or each other.

We don't trust the process, the outcome, who we will be, or what we will recognize of our world when we get there. We don't trust we'll like it. We don't trust we'll be given the courage to get through the pain and uncertainty of the changes, and come out better off than we are now. We like the idea of the reign of God, but we want to keep what we want to keep when we get there. That brings us to rather an impasse. We are only willing to build the reign of God to the extent we trust God and each other.

We ask people to pay a steep price to follow Christ into an uncertain future rather than try to return to the past. They'll only go as far as they trust us and trust God. The next chapter explores how to apply that trust and use the tools we were given when we were authorized to step into the bully pulpit.

Questions for Reflection

1. How has Jesus built trust with you? How does God build faith, hope, and love? How trustworthy do you find God? Where does God seem to be untrustworthy?
2. In what ways do you know yourself to be trustworthy? Less trustworthy?
3. What perception of your trustworthiness do you believe parishioners hold? In what ways might they perceive you to be less trustworthy?
4. Describe your plan to build trust with your listeners.

What You Need to Know

* The quality and depth of trust dictates the quality and depth of our relationships: God with us, us with God, us with one another.
* Trust and distrust are built on what is witnessed and what is absent from view, and perception trumps all.
* Trust is built from hope, faith, and love.
* We can build trust through intentional practices to diagnose, experiment, and appraise.
* The reign of God can be built to the extent we trust one another.

3

The Bully Pulpit

Referring to his office as president of the United States, Theodore Roosevelt coined the phrase *bully pulpit*, but the phrase is shifting from its original meaning. Today we think of the bully pulpit as a "bully" in "the pulpit"—a brash, arrogant, insecure person who has the crowd's attention to intimidate people into going along with the speaker. But that's not how President Roosevelt meant it. In his day, *bully* meant "great, terrific, or fantastic," as in "Bully for you!" He meant the office of the presidency gave him a wonderful platform, the perfect megaphone to direct people's attention.

We preachers have been given the bully pulpit. If there is nothing else preachers can do in the face of overwhelming change and loss, we can use the bully pulpits we've been given. We have been handed the megaphone. The way we use that megaphone to deliver words has a profound impact on their reception. After hearing our sermon, will listeners exclaim, "Bully for you!" or "You bully!"?

How we deliver the sermon will influence the perception of one or the other, and there needs to be a balance. Too many exclamations of "Bully for you!," and we may rightly lose our credibility through pandering. Too many accusations of "You bully!," and people will feel kicked in the shins one too many times and quit church altogether. Either way, we lose our megaphone. While we can't fully predict what listeners will say, we can make more-educated rather than less-educated guesses, and craft our sermons accordingly so the gospel is heard.

Before we get to the nitty-gritty, let's remember what we're trying to do when we enter our bully pulpit. We want the gospel to be spread to the ends of the earth, right? For that to happen, the gospel needs to be heard. If people tune out or dismiss a sermon because they feel defensive, shamed, or that we're pushing them to pull down their beloved skies, they're less likely to listen. They'll tune us out, open their phones to check social media, or argue with us in their heads. Regardless, they're not hearing the gospel. Our aim, therefore, is to present a challenging message in such a way it receives a fair hearing; that it's taken in, considered, and wrestled with. Not only is trust in God and the preacher a prerequisite to listening to a challenging message, so is the listeners' emotional bandwidth. Deciding how much challenge listeners can take is another critical point of the preacher's discernment.

How Much Can Your Listeners Take?

To decide how to use wisely and effectively the megaphone we've been handed, we need to consider carefully how much our congregations can take. Imagine how it feels to come home after a tough day and your spouse is waiting for you at the door to tell you your kid landed in detention for mouthing off to the teacher. You may not have the wherewithal to listen at that moment. If you're too tired and stressed to deal with it, you might tune out your spouse even though the subject is pressing, or vent your frustration and say something you'll later regret. In that moment you don't have the capacity for more stress; you're filled to the brim already.

Our listeners walk into church with varying degrees of stress, and that affects their capacity to listen to a challenging message. If they're less stressed, they'll have a greater capacity to listen to something difficult; if they're more stressed, their capacity will be diminished. Judging their capacity as accurately as you can will help you decide how to use your bully pulpit to proclaim the gospel so it's heard.

Below are questions in two parts to help you make that judgment. Recognizing, of course, that your listeners are not a monolithic group, you still preach to the whole, so these questions ask you to consider the group in general. The first set of questions considers overall topics and events that may affect your listeners inside and outside church. The second set gets more specific to your congregation. The questions suggest you think in terms of numbers, but if you don't like to use numbers, draw pictures, create a mind map of the evidence you witness, or write a narrative. The point is to gain deeper insights about who your listeners are, not the means used to get there.

Instructions for Part One: Topics and Events

Give a score of one to three for each topic below.

Give a "1" if the congregation is feeling non-anxious, unafraid, willing to engage the topic with creative solutions, and displays no or few symptoms of grief.

Give a "2" if you see some evidence, or sense fear, anxiety, or symptoms of grief when the subject is broached or avoided.

Give a "3" if you see strong evidence, or sense great fear, anxiety, or symptoms of grief when the subject is broached or assiduously avoided.

_____ Climate change

_____ Racism

_____ Human sexuality

_____ Respecting the dignity of every human being (including those in the opposite political party)

_____ Common civility (treating *every* person as Christ, including unpopular church or civic leaders)

_____ Forgiveness

_____ Scriptures that point to a preferential option for the poor

_____ Immigration

_____ Loving your neighbor as yourself

_____ The Beatitudes

_____ Congregations closing their doors

_____ Financial giving to the congregation

_____ The general economy

_____ Political elections

_____ Anxiety regarding declining numbers

_____ Prior misconduct by a congregational leader

_____ Natural disasters

_____ Discord between preacher and listeners

_____ Discord between parishioners

_____ (Others?)

_____ Subtotal for Part One

Part Two: Your Local Context

Some questions below ask you to make a list, so grab a piece of scratch paper or open your computer. Follow the scoring prompts for each question.

_____ How many struggles does your congregation face right now? *(Make a list. If something is causing stress, consider it a struggle. How many things can you think of? Write the number in the blank.)*

_____ In general, these struggles are easy to solve and have a solution ready at hand. *(1 = mostly true; 2 = sometimes true; 3 = rarely true)*

_____ In general, these struggles are taking us into new territory without known solutions. *(1 = never true; 2 = sometimes true; 3 = mostly true)*

_____ How many significant struggles did the congregation face in recent memory? *(Make another list. Write the number in the blank.)*

_____ When discussing struggles at meetings, how often does it turn personal? *(1 = never true; 2 = sometimes true; 3 = usually true)*

(Score the following questions: 1 = never; 2 = rarely; 3 = sometimes; 4 = most of the time; 5 = always.)

How often . . .

_____ do meetings display intense emotion?

_____ do meetings avoid intense emotion that are displayed elsewhere?

_____ do members avoid social and political differences?

_____ do parishioners expect lay leaders to solve parish problems for them?

_____ do parish leaders expect you to solve parish problems?

_____ do you receive pushback for preaching an overtly challenging message?

_____ do you decide not to preach a challenging message because of the pushback you expect?

_____ are "elephants" avoided in meetings?

_____ are opposing views discouraged?

_____ are difficult subjects avoided, deflected, or ignored?

_____ are new, creative possibilities rejected?

_____ does this congregation feel it fails with its efforts?

_____ does the "temperature" (the emotional heat) in the room rise when discussing parish challenges in leadership meetings?

_____ do you estimate parishioners trust you? *(1 = most of the time; 2 = sometimes; 3 = rarely)*

_____ Subtotal for Part Two

_____ Subtotal from Part One

_____ Total score

This final number suggests how stressed—how brittle—your congregation is, or how creative—how transformable—it is. The higher the number, the more brittle it is, and the lower the number, the more transformable it is.

A brittle congregation is highly stressed. The people are anxious, they rarely laugh, and they are probably exhibiting symptoms of grief, including anger, lashing out, withdrawing, isolating, waxing nostalgic, circling the wagons, overreacting, bargaining, making much ado about nothing, targeting you or another leader (or a problem) as *the* problem, and/or displaying passive-aggressive behaviors. In other words, the more brittle they are, the more emotionally fragile they are. The more brittle they are, the less likely they are to take in the gospel they don't want to hear—that some parts of the sky are already falling, and others need to be pulled down. They are not ready to hear this because they're too busy insisting the pieces of the sky can, should, and will be held up, and they fuss at you when you don't help them do it. A brittle congregation is also likely to be suspicious of "hidden political agendas" in anything said from your bully pulpit. A brittle congregation can hear only a very few overtly challenging sermons, and only very occasionally.

Conversely, the lower the number, the more prepared they are to be transformed more closely into Christ. These people are more receptive and spiritually flexible. They are able to look at the piece of sky you hand them and examine it with humility and curiosity. They're willing to accept a jagged piece and get cut with truth. Secure in their identity as a child of God, they're ready to see the wrongs they have done, and the rights left undone. They have enough spiritual and emotional trust to accept Christ's forgiveness and amend their lives. They're ready to express gratitude for the way their piece of sky has served them well, but they also see it's time to bury it. They know the particular shade of blue can't be replaced, and they're ready to lament and consider a new sky with a new shade. They are willing to be transformed to resemble the living Christ more closely, even if it hurts at first.

Based on these descriptions, look at your numbers again. Do they seem accurate? Would you adjust your totals up or down? Overall, how brittle or transformable do you believe your congregation to be? How much challenge can they take?

Projecting Our Voices from the Bully Pulpit

Keeping in mind how much our congregations can tolerate, we need to decide how best to use the bully pulpit we've been given. While visual aids and music are used by some preachers, we all use words. Our words are our power tools, and like any tools, we need to understand how to apply them skillfully in service of those who authorized us to use them.

How do we understand these power tools? Imagine this scenario: At the worship service at which you are installed as the congregation's preacher, a member of the congregation hands you a heavy box labeled: "Power Tools: Words! For preacher's use only. Use with caution!" Later, when you unpack the box and open the official user's manual, you read the introduction. It begins:

> Congratulations, Preacher! You have been entrusted with the enclosed power tools of words. To wield these words safely and effectively, the wise user begins by understanding the nature of the power these tools depend on that you have been authorized to employ. Specifically, the power authorized to the preacher by the Holy Spirit and the consent of the congregation is to apply the force of words over time to invite the human spirit to move a certain distance toward the gospel. The preacher, therefore, applies these power tools in three distinct ways: force, distance, and time. Skillful application requires careful practice.

Force: Strength and Pace

Force is neutral even though we often think of "force" as "forceful"—aggressive, pushy, and intrusive. Force might be these things, but not necessarily. The gentle force of a small stream of water can erode mountains; a whisper can be more attention-grabbing than a shout; a sustained cello chord at a pianissimo can move more people to tears than an orchestra playing a torrent of notes. Force just is. It's the application and strength of force that makes the difference.

Preachers have been authorized to use the application and strength of force with our words, by mimicking the application and strength of force God applies to words. God most often uses forceful words of mercy, love, forgiveness, creation, unity, and justice. Just as God does, preachers must decide the force of words to apply in a sermon, choosing along a continuum of gently pastoral to "brook no dissent" prophetic.

We choose the force of our words, for instance, when we choose between God *says* or God *demands*; God *gazes* or God *scrutinizes*; God *discerns* or God *judges*. God also *invites* and *requires*, gives *choices* and *ultimatums*, offers *hope* and *expectations*. Each word choice contains an application and strength of force that will be heard differently, and neither end of the continuum is less effective than the other.

Force is also about pacing. Preaching at a brusque pace is heard very differently than the force of preaching told "slant." We can be brusque and blunt by opening a sermon with, "Today we're talking about climate change, and it's all our fault." Conversely, we might open the curtains slowly over several paragraphs with the gist of, "I'm a gardener. Every year I make a note when the first flowers of spring bloom. I've been delighted each year it's been a little earlier. Or should I be so delighted?"

The pace we choose to force the sermon's message will be felt differently. I'll never forget a masterfully paced sermon my seminary professor gave with the application and strength of force unfolding slowly. His words started like a low rumble of an approaching summer thunderstorm when you can feel the growing tension of the electricity in the air. The sermon used words to build so much tension, when he finally let loose with his thesis it was with all the force of the storm breaking overhead. By that point he had built so much tension so skillfully and slowly, I physically felt the release of the pent-up tension in the air when he thundered out his main point.

Force contains both word choices and the pace at which we apply them. Choose each on the basis of what your listeners can take in. The more brittle the congregation, the less force and the slower the pace that might be needed. The more transformable, the stronger the force and faster the pace they can hear.

Applying Force

The application of force is one of the areas I hear many preachers be intolerant with one another. I hear preachers who apply strongly forceful words when preaching about injustice and judge other preachers as "not doing their jobs" when they choose to apply a gentler, slower, but relentless force to their words. When colleagues judge each other about the "right" type of force to be used, trust is eroded between us, and that affects our relationships beyond preaching. We need each other, especially when preaching during these uncertain times. We need to trust that our colleagues know what their listeners can take more than we armchair quarterback preachers do. We need more humility and more curiosity about how colleagues answer the questions above about their congregation, as well as less condemnation and more offers of support. So, I . . . (choose which strength of force most moves you) . . . suggest . . . invite you to consider . . . strongly urge . . . ask you to reread Matthew 7:1–3. Whichever works for you, please do it; collegial condemnation is more hurtful than many realize.

Distance: Moving toward the Gospel

What do you believe is the gospel? In one sentence, how would you describe it? For example, I believe the good news is God's love, mercy, justice, and compassion are applied equally to every human being, and that through Jesus Christ nothing, not even death, can separate us from God. That's my bottom line, and I am conscious that I read Scripture through that lens. I also perpetually ask God's forgiveness for the gaps I see in myself for not living that good news as completely as the Spirit makes me able.

If my bottom-line belief about the gospel is seen as the "forest," then one Sunday's text is a "tree" in that forest. It's a story in which I discover the specific contours of the gap in my spirit between me and the good news. I am shown the ways I favor my own will instead of God's. For instance, I know if I consented to let the Spirit transform me until my spirit is indistinguishable from Christ's, I would apply God's love, mercy, justice, and compassion to every human being equally. I would live and serve fearlessly, because if nothing can separate me from God, then I have nothing to fear. But I don't consent. I hold back all the time. That gap is the distance the Spirit hopes to move me until my spirit is indistinguishable from Christ's spirit. At that point, it will no longer be I who live, but Christ who lives in me.

To apply this to our sermon prep, compare the implicit and explicit Christian values the congregation holds with its actions. First, conduct an audit about the explicit values the congregation states it holds. What is the congregation's mission statement? What slogans does the congregation use in its web and print advertising? What are the congregational buzzwords? How do parishioners describe the energy and purpose of the congregation?

That's what they say. Now, what is observed? These are the unstated, implicit values held. On a weekly, monthly, and annual basis, what do parishioners do? How do they conduct themselves? How do they talk, give, serve, gesture, participate, look outward, and look inward? Does anyone outside the congregation know the congregation exists, why it exists, or what's inside? What are the demographics of the congregation, not only in terms of ethnicity, sexual orientation, economic and educational status, and so on, but social and political leanings? How does this mirror the surrounding neighborhood?

Compare the lists. Do the explicitly stated beliefs about the gospel match the parishioners' implicit, observable behaviors? The gap between them suggests the distance God invites them to move toward the gospel.

Finally, look at the parish system. What in the system is created and maintained to achieve the gap? Jeff Lawrence said, "There is no such thing as a dysfunctional organization, because every organization is perfectly aligned to achieve the results it currently gets."[1] For instance, one system in which many of us are complicit, is fostering congregations based more on agreement on political and social issues than on spreading the gospel. Indeed, we are more likely to characterize a congregation by the color of their politics than by the Christ-like acts of their compassion. We're so tired of dealing with the disagreements in the world, we need a refuge, a haven, a safe space to let our guard down and be fed so we can go back out there. It's understandable we look for a "liberal" or "conservative" church, or "traditional values" to match our own.

However, this means we choose a church deliberately to feel like we belong to our "tribe" based on common political agreement, than our common identity as baptized believers. We want to find reinforcement and reassurance about what we already believe about the world. We seek social and gospel proof that we've chosen rightly. On that basis, many of our congregations build walls of inclusion and exclusion that are systemically entrenched.

We have moved from accusing Jesus of being unclean if he dines with sinners and prostitutes—we're good with that—to accusing each other of being unclean if we dine with, sincerely pray for, or welcome those who hold the opposite social or political viewpoint. Jesus invited Matthew, a tax collector who colluded willingly and knowingly with the Roman taxation system of his fellow Jews, into his inner circle. Matthew had actively engaged in, and profited from, a heinous system of oppression and brutality against his own people. How many coins had his fellow Jews placed in Matthew's palms that later were placed in the palms of a carpenter—to cut the beams of wood used to form execution crosses? How many of those coins, stamped with Caesar's image, the image of the state, were used to pay the wages of the soldiers on duty the day orders were given to nail Jesus of Nazareth to one of those carpenter's crosses? Where do we draw our own lines in the sand between who is welcomed and who isn't, who is invited into the parish's inner circles and who isn't, and who belongs and who doesn't? (*As a teachable moment, how does my choice of strongly forceful words and their pace in this paragraph sit with you? How might your congregation hear such words?*)

If your congregation claims to be welcoming, for instance, but everyone pretty much looks, talks, and believes like each other—and you'd guess votes like each other too—what might that suggest? When, where, and how are they actively spreading the gospel beyond their safe walls of respite? If the rationale is that the neighborhood or region is monolithic so there's "no one" to invite, is that a true story? If it is, it begs the question why the neighborhood would be monolithic to begin with. What's the history behind the area and the core systems in place that make it what it is? Again, how much distance separates the congregation's stated beliefs in the gospel, and what you observe?

That gap is the distance the Spirit hopes to close between gospel and people. That distance also suggests how brittle or transformable the congregation is, as well as how much distance is needed for the Spirit to move them, in part, through sermons. As Joan Chittiser, OSB, wrote, "We cannot not change. But we can refuse to be converted."[2] Our job as preachers is not to convert people to the gospel; only an accord between the person and the Spirit can do that. Our job is to issue the invitation to conversion over and over. We invite as skillfully as we can in the hopes it will be received, with faith that the Spirit is at work and wants conversion more than we do. We preach with love, compassion, and empathy knowing listeners are free to exercise their free will to say, "Yes, the gospel's a great idea, let's go," or "Nuh-uh, I'm not budging."

Time: How Much Is Available?

The force of our words, and the distance between gospel and us, is also influenced by the amount of time we have to preach. Water has had millions of years to gently but relentlessly carve the Grand Canyon. In other circumstances, water needed only seconds to unleash a massive amount of stored force in a tsunami, violently carving a town away from its mainland in moments. The effects of the force of our words depends just as much on the length of time they're applied as on their strength. It's likely the longer the distance there is to overcome, and the more brittle the congregation, the more time will be required to move them.

Let me here offer my hope that you don't admit discouragement if you don't immediately witness visible change in those to whom you preach. In my work with preachers, I hear many wonder what they're doing wrong—or what they're doing at all. They feel that if their listeners' hearts and minds aren't changing, then it must be their fault. Not at all! Again, the further the distance and the more brittle the congregation's spirit, (unless they have a "Paul on the road to Damascus" moment), the more likely they will require a relentless, but gentle trickle of the Spirit. More force, and they'll "break," either by tuning out, leaving the congregation, trying to get you to leave, or using other deflecting behaviors. In other words, the change required may take longer than you will have in their bully pulpit, even if no one ever tries to run you out on a rail. Take heart, and be of good courage: it could take decades or longer for them to move. After all, we're two thousand years post-resurrection, and the Spirit is still preaching the same things to us over and over!

To put this in perspective, imagine if you were to preach the first Sunday of your new call, but never again. Even if that one sermon were extraordinarily powerful and memorable, what do you imagine the long-term effects would be on moving your listeners toward the gospel? I'm guessing that one sermon wouldn't "move the needle" very far. If it could, then Jesus literally wasted his breath to preach as often as he did; one sermon would have sufficed! If one sermon wasn't enough for Jesus to accomplish his aims, who's to know how many we need to preach? We can only make an educated guess.

I mean this literally: we can make an educated guess to be realistic about how much we can afford to focus on a particular theological topic over time. The number of Sundays we have available in the bully pulpit is precious and requires planning.

How many Sunday and Holy Week sermons do you preach when most of the assembly will be gathered? There are fifty-two Sundays, plus Maundy Thursday and Good Friday, which makes fifty-four. Subtract the Sundays you're gone for continuing education (two), retreat (one), guest preachers (two), and vacation (four). If you're a solo pastor, you're down to forty-five. It will be fewer if the pulpit is shared with an associate.

Look back at the scores from the beginning of the chapter that guesstimated the brittleness and transformability of the congregation. Now let's say the writing is on the wall about the congregation's ability to afford to keep its church doors open. Unless there's a massive infusion of steady income (which could happen; the Holy Spirit has done stranger things), you believe they need to build their trust in God. No matter what happens to the church building, they need to trust in God's faithfulness to them, hope in a future they cannot yet imagine, and believe God loves and sees them no matter where they are. In other words, they need help to detach spiritually and emotionally from the building, and their identities, roles, and relationships in relation to it. It's time for the congregation to write a living will, and plan the funeral for the building and the congregation as they have known it, before it's a crisis.

If you discerned they are a brittle, highly anxious congregation, and you have observed this anxiety especially about the building, they probably couldn't hear an "in your face" sermon about giving up the building. This means a slow and steady gentle force of words over a long period of time is needed to move them the distance required to accept the inevitable, and trust a new sky is being painted.

How might you do this? Starting with forty-five sermons for the year, you could plan a summer preaching series of eight sermons about trust: what it is, what it isn't, how to build it in each other, and how to understand God trusts them. A few weeks later in the fall, you could focus on the mission of the congregation, its history, when God has been abundantly evident, and how they got through when God seemed disconcertingly absent. Then, during Advent, you could focus on hope, anticipation, and the difficulty of waiting for God's promises to be revealed. Epiphany could explore faith in the many ways God surprises us by showing up in the real world, in real time, in ways beyond our imagining. Lent might be the time to coordinate your preaching with Christian education aimed at preparing for our deaths individually—and as a congregation—and lamenting the things we hold dear that pass away. Easter, of course, is the promise and joy of unexpected, new life, and that no matter what, God always has another chapter to write for the congregation's story.

Over the course of a year, then, most of those forty-five available sermons focus on one theological theme: trust in God that there is always new life after death, even the death of a congregation. It also means there may not be sermons available that year to tackle other pressing issues, so change in those areas ought not to be expected. You will have preached the gospel you felt called to preach, while also not bearing more responsibility for the outcome than is yours to bear. You have only so much time in your bully pulpit, and no more. You will have done what you could, so you can let go of what you couldn't. No guilt, no shame, no remorse, no superhero fantasies. You're just a preacher. Did you preach? Did you preach faithfully? Then your job is done, and you can breathe easily and with gratitude for the Spirit's good work.

A question that often arises is how focusing on a theme or subject works for lectionary preachers. First, look ahead in the lectionary to see whether a theological theme jumps out as a natural fit. If not, I'll paraphrase the words of the Episcopal Presiding Bishop Michael Curry: "I know what the text assigned is for today, but in my sanctified imagination, the Holy Spirit wants me to focus on *this* text!" Read the new text, and carry on. Also, don't overlook the Psalms. There is so much emotion and ordinary human experience in them that might be linked to your theme without stretching. You can also ask permission as needed. For example, the Episcopal Church allows preachers to go off lectionary if we get our bishop's permission. Finally, broad theological themes (like trusting God, no matter what) may be less difficult to apply to a given text than you might imagine.

To recap this section, "the power authorized to the preacher by the Holy Spirit and the consent of the congregation is to apply the force of words over time to invite the human spirit to move a certain distance toward the gospel." Force, distance, and time are what we have to work with to employ our words in the bully pulpit, as our congregations authorized us to do. Considered together, we can skillfully craft sermons of good news our listeners don't want to hear but can take in.

Conclusion

We have been given a bully pulpit—a wonderful, extraordinary, grace-filled privilege of a pulpit. Our congregations ask us to use it, and trust us to use it wisely. That megaphone is one of the most powerful tools we're given. By praying over our listeners and asking for the Spirit's guidance, we can discern their capacity—and incapacity—to be transformed into Christ's image. The more accurately we discern this, the more effectively we can apply the tools we have been given. We'll craft our words to assist our listeners not only to hear a gospel they don't want but will wrestle with, and emerge ready to paint a new sky.

Before moving to the next chapter, let's recap where we've been so far. In chapter one, "Letting the Sky Fall," I suggested the essence of a challenging sermon is not the sermon's subject or form, but the relationship the listener has to the pieces of their "sky." Any sermon in which the listener perceives a valued piece of their sky is threatened will feel challenging. Through St. Paul's conversion, we identified the pieces of our skies: roles, systems, identities, well-being, livelihoods, and relationships. We also looked at some ways our grief is exhibited when those pieces fall: we look back, lash out, are possessed by the demon of fear, and lament. Moreover, any piece of the sky that falls means a piece of ourselves dies with it. We lose a bit of our lives, but in exchange—and if we consent—we gain life in Christ.

Chapter two, "Building Mutual Trust," explored the necessity for and components of trust, and how to build them intentionally. When Jesus says we can trust what he says, he means we can trust in God's hope, faith, and love. Moreover, we as preachers can intentionally build trust with our listeners so when our sermons suggest letting pieces of skies fall, people will listen; they will trust we have their best interests at heart. The more trust we build, the more people will listen, even when the message feels challenging.

This chapter, "The Bully Pulpit," examined the authority and tools we were given to preach those challenging messages. Paradoxically, the people who invited us into their pulpits authorized us to preach the gospel they don't want to hear. The bully pulpit grants us a sacred megaphone to project the words that dying always precedes rising. Discerning the brittleness and transformability of our listeners helps us choose wisely the application of our words' force, distance, and time to invite people to move toward Christ.

Before offering suggestions about what to preach in a challenging sermon and how to preach it, we need to answer one more foundational question. Even when listeners trust us, why would they let us guide them to their deaths?

Questions for Reflection

1. *Brittleness and Transformability*
   After discerning the brittleness or transformability of your congregation:

   a. How does this affect your sense of what is realistic to accomplish during your tenure?

   b. How does it affect your enthusiasm for your call to serve them?

   c. How "at home" do you feel among them? What difference does that make personally and professionally?

2. *Force, Distance, and Time*

   a. What's your comfort level with using various levels of force with your words? Consider both strength and pacing.
   b. When you consider the gap between your listeners and the gospel you believe God calls them to live into, what effect does that have on you?
   c. Based on the length of time that may be required for your listeners to be moved closer to the gospel, how does that fit with your sense of responsibility as their preacher? How might it affect your tenure with them?
   d. What planning would help make the best use of the number of sermons you have available to move your listeners in the direction of the gospel? Consider force, distance, and time.

What You Need to Know

* The more brittle a congregation, the more likely it is to break. The more transformable it is, the more flexibility they have to be transformed into the likeness of Christ.
* The power authorized to the preacher by the Holy Spirit and the consent of the congregation is to apply the force of words over time to invite the human spirit to move a certain distance toward the gospel.

4

The Preacher as Trusted Guide

Indeed, there is a mismatch between the change in the pace of change and our ability to develop the learning systems, training systems, management systems, social safety nets, and government regulations that would enable citizens to get the most out of these accelerations and cushion their worst impacts.[1] —Thomas Friedman

Surrender is the crossover point of life. It distinguishes who I was from who I have become. Surrender comes in grand ways and in small ones but, sooner or later, I must admit that there is no turning back from the rejection or the loss or the turn of age or the abandonment. Life as I had fantasized it is ended. What is left is the spiritual obligation to accept reality so that the spiritual life can really happen in me.[2] —Joan Chittister

At the end of the Gospel of John, the post-resurrection Jesus is on the beach with his disciples. He asks Peter, "Do you love me more than these?" Peter says he does. Jesus tells him, "Feed my lambs." Jesus asks him again, "Do you love me?" Peter assures him, "You know I love you." Jesus tells him, "Feed my sheep." Jesus asks a third time, "Do you love me?" Peter feels hurt. Is Jesus questioning that Peter's love for him is capped so he won't risk all for him? That Peter won't be willing to learn as much as he will need to in order to build the future church? That Peter won't demonstrate his love for Jesus reliably and dependably? Or is it that Peter didn't see Jesus for all Jesus was worth? I don't think Jesus was pressing Peter because he didn't trust him. I think he was pressing Peter because Jesus knew what was ahead.

Up to this point, Jesus had been the target for the scoffers, the cynics, the greedy, the holier-than-thou, the petty, and the complacent. When Jesus was no longer in sight, Peter, the rock upon whom the church would be built, would be the target in Jesus's stead. Peter would be on the receiving end of the scoffers, the cynics, the greedy, and the rest. Peter would be the one stirring things up. Peter would be the one to share the news that people had to repent, turn around, let their old ways die, die to self, and be raised again through baptism in order to carry out Jesus's ministry of restoration. Peter would have to contend with promises of Jesus's return that weren't fulfilled as expected. Peter would have to see his efforts appear to go unrewarded. Peter would have to suffer. Jesus questioned Peter because Jesus knew what was ahead, and he knew how easy it would be for Peter to lose his way.

Jesus presses Peter to love him more than these because fear could make Peter forget the mission; after all, Peter was only human. Jesus places an earworm on endless loop in Peter's head to carry him through the decisions, the uncertainty, the weariness, the relationships he would lose, and the loneliness. "Don't forget, Peter," Jesus urges. "Love me more than these. Love me more than your relationships. Love me more than your comfort. Love me more than your safety. Love me more than your life. Love me more than all these."

To love Jesus more than these requires us to perpetually let fall from the sky everything we love more than Jesus: our relationships, our self-identity, our expectations, our hopes that favor us above others, our systems, our safety, and our very lives. We wander about in uncertainty as we learn to love Jesus, whom we touch, hear, and see only by inference and interpretation, more than we love the world we can touch, hear, and see, and more than we love self-preservation.

When we focus our mission where it belongs, to love Jesus more than these and tend his sheep, hope is realized. What we long for is fulfilled. As we orient toward Christ, we are filled with comfort: our hearts are strengthened. When our hearts are strengthened, we are filled and go out with courage. Now we know why we need to look for solutions to the huge challenges we face, because Jesus's sheep are being affected adversely. They're hurting. We love Jesus. Jesus loves his sheep—and doesn't want them to hurt.

Preachers aren't charged with solving the whole problem but to do the next one thing we can: feed a sheep, tend a lamb, love them more. Make sure Jesus's flock knows they are respected, that they matter, that we're in this together, that we'll work together to clean up our common messes no matter who made them, that God loves and forgives them. That's how we fulfill our mission. When we love this mission more than all else, the rest will follow.

It may feel impossible, though, for the rest to follow. How do we incarnate the mission to love Jesus's sheep with respect, forgiveness, and justice? With God's help. With God's help, we will do infinitely more than we can ask or imagine. With God's help, God's reign will get built, though we must pay a worthwhile price for the parts and labor. The price is to die to self, so we love Christ even more than this.

Dying, it turns out, isn't so bad after all. Preach it.

With so much change and so much dying yet to come, why will anyone listen to preachers? Why will parishioners let us guide them to their own graves where they don't want to go? What will help listeners trust they really will be okay if the sky falls? By preaching Jesus is the way, the truth, and the life.

Jesus Is the Way: Guiding Your Church to Fulfill Its Mission

Just as Jesus asked Peter, Jesus asks us to love Jesus first and most. This requires us to let fall from the sky everything we love more than Jesus. As leaders standing in Peter's stead, we'll have to figure out what this means on the fly in a changing world, just as he did. The mission of the church describes true north.

"Q. What is the mission of the Church?

A. The mission of the Church is to restore all people to unity with God and each other in Christ.

Q. How does the Church pursue its mission?

A. The Church pursues its mission as it prays and worships, proclaims the gospel, and promotes justice, peace, and love.

Q. Through whom does the Church carry out its mission?

A. The Church carries out its mission through the ministry of all its members."[3]

This is the mission of the church as Episcopalians understand it, but your denomination is probably similar. Christianity's common ground is our hope to restore everything to unity with God and each other. No news there. But do you notice what's missing? Results. It's in the pursuit of restoration that our mission is fulfilled. Our mission is the means, not the end. When our attention is fixed on the means, the end—restoration—will be the result.

Moreover, if we feel discouraged when we don't see the results of our efforts, that's about us, not about fulfilling the mission. If we get discouraged because we're not "producing," that means we've shifted from "Jesus is the way" to "Results are the way," "Proving ourselves is the way," or "Trying to save the church singlehandedly is the way."

When we refocus our mission where it belongs, to love Jesus most, we are filled with comfort and strengthened with courage to tend his sheep. Because Jesus's sheep are affected as they watch their skies fall, we see them hurting. Jesus sees them hurting, and we are to tend them on his behalf. We aren't charged with solving the world's problems, nor are we charged to "fix" anyone's falling skies. But when we stick to our missional "lane" and relentlessly and perpetually pursue our mission, Christ will manage the rest.

Looking at the specifics, then, our mission says if we are praying, we are achieving what we are charged to achieve. If we are worshipping, we are achieving what we are charged to achieve. If we are proclaiming the gospel, and if we are promoting, contributing to, and fostering justice, peace, and love, we are achieving what we are charged to achieve.

Living in a data-driven, results-oriented culture which I see influencing the church more and more, this feels almost heretical. Why aren't outcomes our mandate? Why aren't we charged to get results? Because justice, peace, and love require conversion.

Each of these requires a conversion of heart, a change of identity, a change of systems, roles, and livelihoods. They all require giving up self for Christ. No preacher can persuade people's hearts that Jesus has their best interests in his heart. We can invite them to trust that Jesus does, but only God, with their hearts' consent, can finally persuade and convert them. When we know that Jesus is the way, we know the mission of the church is to *invite* by offering prayer, worship, and proclamation without ceasing, and by seeking justice promotes the dignity of every human being, but the act of conversion to restoration and unity is God's purview.

Only God can create restoration. Our job as preachers is to make saying yes to the pain of change and conversion sound irresistible.

Jesus Is the Truth: Guiding Your Church through Grief and Lamentation

We think we shouldn't have to grieve. There should be a way around death. The world as we have known and loved it shouldn't have to die. And yet the truth is, we as a nation and a world are slowly gathering on a Golgotha filled with crosses. We are watching those things we love get nailed to them—coastlines, jobs, and our clergy stipends; "my tribe," diluted by mixing with another "tribe"; polar bears, whose white icebergs of safety have melted, and coral reefs warmed to dead white; California hillsides that burn while human civility is going up in flames; confidence in cars, satellites, electrical grids, and voting booths subverted by super-smart hackers who sink our super-vulnerable computers; and faith in the church as pews empty out.

Big, big sigh. This is going to be hard work. Hard, necessary, blessed, holy work. Where do we even start? The same place we start when a parishioner tells us their loved one has just been moved to hospice. However, since it's unlikely someone will say, "I'm mourning because the church I grew up in is on its deathbed and probably only has hours to live" (or similar such sentiments), we listen for the clues that indicate someone is experiencing or fearing a loss. For example:

* I don't know how we got here.
* I don't recognize this world I'm in.
* I never thought this would happen.
* I just don't understand.
* My family members and I split over politics.
* We have to protect our way of life.
* This isn't the country I knew.
* I don't know where I belong.
* What happened to my church?
* How will I feed my kids?

When you hear clues like these, move into pastoral care mode. If the situation permits, ask what changed, and listen for the types of loss they're describing: systems, well-being, roles, self-identity, and especially changes in relationships. Ask, for example:

* What have they lost, or what do they fear losing?
* What were their expectations?
* What do they imagine the future holds?
* What are their hopes for their loved ones?
* What do they fear might not happen for them?
* How is the change affecting them?

Listen for intransigence: an unwillingness to admit all things come to an end, or these changes can only happen over their dead body. Listen to get a sense of their trust in God that death is not the end.

* Where is God in the midst of these changes?
* Where does God seem to be active?
* Where does God seem to be absent?
* Do they feel God is faithful to them?
* Does God see, care about, and seem present with their pain and fear?
* Do they have hope?
* What do they expect of God?
* What do they hope God does?
* What if it doesn't turn out that way?

By asking questions, people have the chance to articulate their experience, wrestle with their theology, and find out where they see their beloved in the dying process. Do they see their beloved in the early stages, when perhaps it could still be turned around? Is it at the midpoint when it's comfort measures only? Perhaps the family is gathered and waiting for the last, final breaths and wondering if you could come pray with them. Or maybe they can say out loud their loved one is gone—and isn't coming back. Of course, they may not know whether their beloved is actually dying. It may be too early to tell, and uncertainty is stressful. They may feel anticipatory fear for the grief ahead they can't name yet. As you listen, pay attention to clues that suggest their brittleness or transformability.

Help them see themselves in the scriptural narrative. Help them see themselves in the scriptural narrative; which biblical characters would empathize with them? In addition, let them know they're not alone, lots of things are changing all at once, these changes are really hard, and we're in this together. Let them know you see them. While you're extending compassion, you're also building the trust you'll need when you preach a challenging message.

In addition to sensitive pastoral care and preaching, we need creative liturgists to craft rituals for real and symbolic deaths that don't have bodies to bury, in the way "blue Christmas" liturgies have done, and liturgies for divorce, or the decommissioning of a church building. For example, many were hit hard by the Great Recession. What might a ritual have looked like to help people lament what they lost, including their foreclosed homes, a mortgage and government system that let them down, and the dreams of their retirement dissolved with lost pension funds? Or what would a liturgy look like to name, give thanks, and let the sky fall on "the way things used to be," like full pews, and abundant church programs and staffs; the career for which someone trained that artificial intelligence has rendered obsolete; or the home in California wiped out because of one of the many intensifying wildfires? Moreover, we need rituals in which we surrender "the way things ought to be," like the world we thought we were giving our children.

Creating a twist on South Africa's Truth and Reconciliation Commission, we need Truth and Lamentation Commissions. It's hard, messy work to tell the truth about what is passing and what's ahead. It's harder, messier work to grieve. It's going to be extremely difficult to be compassionate and courageous enough to stay with people's unique feelings of loss over things others find ridiculous, petty, or abhorrent. This brings me to one of the hardest, scariest things I have to say in this book, and I hope I have built enough trust in you by now to do so: how do we help white people through their feelings of loss?

It is way past time for white privilege and power to lose their supremacy. But since loss is experienced because of the relationship one has to the thing being lost, and as human migration changes the complexion and power structures of towns and cities across the US, some white people feel increasingly threatened because they won't be in control as often; they won't recognize their town; they won't know where they belong; and they'll wonder whether they—and those they love—are safe. White people's fear for their safety is a deep-seated, emotional, irrational response. It isn't fair, it isn't accurate, and it's a sign in itself of white privilege and supremacy that these are the questions some white people fear and face. People of color have always lived this reality and can't escape it. It isn't right.

White people are not telling themselves a true story about their fears, but they believe the story they're telling themselves, nonetheless. It's *their relationship* to what they fear that is being lost, and that loss is as true and real to them as anyone else's losses are, as real as the loss of cat fourteen of seventeen is to the cat lady. They know this change is inevitable. They also know their conversion is not. That's why they're so defensive and going on the offensive.

As a white person myself, by suggesting pastoral sensitivity to white people's fear of and grief for their losses, I don't want to appear that I believe those fears are justified, the losses are not, or that these changes are not demanded by the gospel. But here's my big concern if we don't acknowledge white people's fear and loss. If we say their losses don't matter, that it's high time they lost power and should get over it, they'll feel shamed, isolated, and backed into a corner—and, I fear, act out accordingly, as we see a growing number doing now. While these changes are underway, the fear, grief, and subsequent behaviors will get worse before they get better, and the sins of the parents will be bestowed on (at least some of) their children. If the church doesn't help them see the death they fear as inevitable *but not the end*, and a new shade of blue sky a blessing, how else can we hope for them to surrender their false gods of superiority? How else can they die to self and be open to conversion and genuine resurrection, so they rise up to see all people as God's beloved children? We have to leave open a way out, a way through, a way back.

At the same time, we need that Truth and Lamentation Commission for people of color and all oppressed people to speak their truth, lament, and, because reconciliation demands it, tell their oppressors what "amendment of life" requires. There are many, many layers to the systems we've created and are complicit in maintaining because they benefit those in power. There are many layers to the generations of wounds, losses, and actual deaths to people of color and underrepresented groups. There's much to mourn and much from which to rise.

I do not have answers. But I and we are part of a mission: to seek and preach reconciliation. We belong to a church that can excel at holding pastoral conversations, and is filled with theologically creative people who can bring to life Truth and Lamentation Commissions to craft healing liturgies and rituals of dialogue. We belong to a church that, on its holiest days, exhibits holy courage for hard conversations, tears, and divine courage to begin again.

Jesus is the way and the truth, so do not be afraid: the world and church as we have known them are passing away, and not coming back. As we transition from one life to the next, it will hurt, and it will be messy, and we will grieve—but truth is hope. Telling the truth, all of it, to each other, from the beginning, is required to love these more.

Jesus Is the Life: Guiding Your Church to Recognize Its Identity

When asked to describe themselves, most people (myself included) begin in terms of either their primary relationships (girlfriend, wife, mother, boyfriend, husband, father) or their careers (priest, pastor, doctor, teacher, barista, student). When we hear someone describe themselves this way, it gives us a sense of what they feel is most important about themselves.

This response is natural. It's knee-jerk. We locate ourselves in the context of others. We place ourselves among the people we cherish and the efforts we give ourselves to. It's *ubuntu,* the Nguni word that translates roughly to, "I am, because we are." I am, because I know myself in relation to us. I am, because I am in relation to people, ideas, home, education, family, expectations, dreams, pets, memories, and patterns of nature. I am, because we are in relationship.

We also demonstrate who we are by our sense of value from the work we produce. The fruits of our labors let us be seen. Our work makes something exist outside of ourselves and shows we contributed, that we mattered. In other words, we describe ourselves by what is incarnated. We describe ourselves by what someone else could see, touch, hear, and verify. We know ourselves by the tangible extensions others can validate and agree on: we are here.

To talk about relationships and work is a common language in American culture—as common as talking about the weather—because they hold the possibility of connection. Every person on the planet is related to someone else; even if their relatives are deceased, and even if they don't know who they were, they came from a mom and dad. Moreover, nearly everyone on the planet knows their subsistence must come from somewhere, and for the vast majority, their subsistence comes from their work. Relationships and work are categories people relate to, and when described by two people, common ground is established. A relationship is begun or deepened.

Remember, it's the attachment to, and the value we place in, a relationship that causes the problems. All of us are uniquely and individually attached to our pieces of the sky that reflect our understanding of who we are. When a piece falls, many of us don't recognize we're feeling a deep, inarticulate, and unidentified angst and fear. Each piece that falls when a loved one dies, when technology leaps, when a new type of person shows up in a formerly homogeneous town, when a haze of smoke heralds the onset of fire season, when a church program is not renewed . . . each perceived loss raises existential questions: if this thing changes, what becomes of us? Who are we as a people? Who is my tribe? Where do I belong? Am I safe? And finally, who am I?

Here's one woman's vivid experience when her "I" was shattered when her "we" fell from the sky. This moment, recorded in Dani Shapiro's memoir, *Inheritance: A Memoir of Genealogy, Paternity, and Love*, describes the tipping point when the author surrendered her last shred of confirmation bias, and accepted the truth that her beloved deceased father was not her biological father. "I slipped out of bed and walked barefoot into the bathroom. My mind and body seemed to be disconnected. My body wasn't the body I had believed it to be for fifty-four years. My face wasn't my face. That's what it felt like. If my body wasn't my body and my face wasn't my face, who was I?"[4]

For Christians, our nearly universal mistake is to fabricate our "face"—our identity—more from someone or something than from Christ. We make our identity out of relationships that are temporal more than from the relationship that is eternal, more from the things that change, instead of from the only thing that cannot be shaken. Through Christ's death and resurrection, we are baptized children of God. That is our real face. That is our true identity. That is our life.

I'm not sure we in the mainline church—or at least not the particular churches of which I have been a part—do a great job of helping us live into our first, foundational, unshakable, eternal identity as baptized children of God. How would you respond if a person introduced himself this way: "I'm a baptized, beloved, eternal child of God, and attend St. Swithens-by-the-Sea. Because I love Jesus, I spend my days tending his sheep." Uhh . . . the response would probably be stunned silence followed by a rapid exit. (Or is that just me?)

More to the point, what would happen if we first thought of ourselves this way? What if we really did locate our minds, hearts, spirits, choices, and actions not on things temporal but on things eternal? What if we didn't store up—make idols of— "treasures on earth where moth and rust consume and where thieves break in and steal?" What would happen if we arranged our days to store up for ourselves "treasures in heaven, where neither moth nor rust consumes and where thieves do not break in and steal?" (Matt 6:19–20).

If we did, our hearts would be more fixed on what is eternal. They would rest on that which does not and cannot be changed. We would know ourselves first in relationship to God. We would trust God sees us, we matter to God, and our temporary relationships and our work are offered in service to our mission to tend Jesus's sheep.

That's not the same as saying we will be unfeeling when temporary relationships end. When we lose someone or something we love, it will hurt. Though Jesus knew better than anyone that his relationship to his Father was eternal, Jesus still wept when his friend Lazarus died, right? But when we stand on the church's one foundation of Jesus Christ our Lord, our losses contain context and perspective. We learn perpetually that who we are in relation to others nuances and colors our self-understanding and identity, but is not the genesis of it. Indeed, our permanent, true name, the name by which we could most accurately introduce ourselves, is "Child of God."

When we know who we are unalterably, we trust we *can* live without the person or thing we love, as Joan Chittister says. "Life as I had fantasized it is ended. What is left is the spiritual obligation to accept reality so that the spiritual life can really happen in me."[5] When we surrender what was, or what we thought was, or what we thought would be or should be, Jesus becomes our life and we are converted. We store treasures in heaven that can be spent well on Jesus's sheep while we're still on earth.

Conclusion

This is a big part of our work as the church: to reclaim the primacy of our identity as children of God. Not only because we've let our identities be co-opted by the culture and our egos, and not only because it's true, but because it's the reality we need to cling to and move with if we are to weather the days ahead in service to Jesus's sheep. Our world and church have a whole lot of dying to self ahead, and that means we have to make a choice. We can either scatter to the four winds like the disciples did from Jesus after the Last Supper, or we can be courageous and faithful, and draw comfort from each other like the women who stood at the foot of the cross. Like the women, we need to cry and lament until our bodies are spent with grief. It's going to be exhausting to endure, and painful and ugly to watch.

During that time, our self-understanding will take a beating. We'll grasp at straws to hang onto our sense of self, to meaning, to systems we think will protect us, and to relationships with people, places, and patterns. We're probably going to make some really good creative decisions—and some really big, really dumb ones— and we're also going to have to clean up each others' messes.

As we enter this second reformation of a church being released from its buildings, programs, and budgets, I see the most important mission of the church is to encourage conversion of dying to self, so we're available to love Christ and his sheep first and most. I heard someone ask recently why we as a church are standing around wringing our hands in the mortuary when we need to move out to the light. My answer is, it's because we know we're not ready for the light—not until we've buried the bodies. We're standing in the mortuary because we're waiting for someone to prepare the bodies, and plan for and invite us to the service. Until then, we're stuck wringing our hands, waiting to say good-bye. We can't move. As we enter this new reformation, the primary mission of the church is to prepare the metaphorical bodies of the world and church that are passing away, tell the truth, create the liturgies, and call people to honor and celebrate the deceased, so we *can* move into the light of resurrection.

Questions for Reflection

1. What and whom do you love more than "these"?
2. What do you fear losing if you die to self?
3. How is Jesus the way? What is the mission where you serve? What is the mission for you in your vocation?

4. How is Jesus the truth? What truth needs to be spoken aloud, lamented? What truth do you fear to say out loud? To hear? What gives you the courage to do so?
5. How is Jesus the life? How do you describe yourself in relation to others? How would it affect you to lose those relationships? How do you derive your identity? When and how was it shaken? How was it restored?

What You Need to Know

* The world is changing more and at a faster rate than at any time in human history. That means a lot of change, loss, and grief.
* People will trust preachers to guide them to the grave when we preach Jesus is the way, the truth, and the life.
* The church's current, urgent mission is to talk through and ritualize Good Friday for as long as it takes, until we are clear-hearted enough to rise on Easter Sunday.

5

Sermon Approaches

Below are eleven approaches to apply the tools of our words to craft challenging messages. Of course, add your own to the list.

1. "I am persuaded."

"For I am persuaded . . . that neither death nor life . . . nor anything else in all creation can separate us from the love of God in Christ Jesus our Lord" (Rom 9:37–39). This is one of Paul's most famous lines from his letters and an often-quoted one; it's certainly one of my favorites.

Preaching is the art of communicating the Spirit's desire to persuade listeners that they are loved and forgiven more than they realize. It is the art of persuading listeners to believe something they didn't before; and then they are converted. They can go into the world unafraid to see what they have been blinded to before, and work to change what is awry when others are not being treated as lovingly as they know God loves them.

To be persuaded about anything means we're less persuaded, or no longer persuaded at all, by what we used to believe. Something new has come to light. We have new information, new evidence, a new experience that shifts our hearts and thinking. When weighed against each other, the new understanding makes more sense than the previous one. To be persuaded also suggests implicitly that we're still learning, we're still open, and there might be new evidence yet to come to persuade us to still another, deeper understanding. Consider again what happened to Paul. It's a gross understatement to say he was persuaded to change the entire course of his life!

To say in a sermon that we are persuaded opens a dialogue. We admit we're offering our best conclusion to this point while also suggesting new insights might change our minds. In other words, we don't necessarily know "better" than our listeners. In fact, we're saying our listeners might know better than we do, and we're willing to be persuaded by them and their insights, wisdom, knowledge, and experience.

This requires risk and vulnerability on our part, and it points to the kind of trust we're building. We see and value our listeners. We're willing to learn from them. We're sincere when we describe what has persuaded us—and we're open to being persuaded by them further still.

2. Create a sermonic arc.

Music "goes" somewhere. Hear in your inner ear the hymn "Amazing Grace." The tune is constructed like a contemporary two-episode TV show. You know that long note on "me," at the end of ". . . who saved a wretch like me-e-e-e-?" That long note concludes the "first episode" with a cliffhanger: that note is unresolved. It's like a question asked without giving the answer. It begs for another note to follow, another episode to answer the question. We begin the second episode, "I once was lost . . ." and keep singing until it lands on the final note of the two-part series, ". . . was blind, but now I see-e-e-e." Ahhh, the resolution of the plot. The tune concludes, resolving the cliffhanger left over from episode one. Question answered; we can go in peace!

Musicians know this doesn't happen by accident. Musicians know music starts us in one place and takes us to another with a musical arc. In fact, musicians often draw long arc lines from one measure to another many measures away to keep in mind every note played is taking us to that landing spot.

Preachers do this in a single sermon. We begin in one place and take our listeners to a new place. The sermon "lands." One common way this happens is when the conclusion wraps back to the beginning to tie the whole thing into a neat bow. We feel that satisfying "Ahhh" when the sermon concludes, resolving the tension. This is analogous to a tune when the musical arc is short, like "Amazing Grace."

This same idea can be used over a longer sermonic arc, akin to an orchestral composition with several movements but one theme explored throughout. What's the longer journey you want to take your listeners on? What's a theme that needs more time to develop with several episodes and cliffhangers before it finally resolves?

For instance, consider the lived theology of the congregation compared to the gospel. A great example is that church legend about the preacher who gave the same sermon every single week: love your neighbor like yourself. When the parishioners demanded to know why she didn't preach another message, she responded, "Because you haven't heard the first one yet." The lived theology of that congregation was not a loving one, though their stated theology was. What's the lived theology of the congregation? How do they behave toward each other and you? How do they behave toward the parish staff, including the nonprofessional staff and parish secretary? How do they behave toward the neighbors around the church, and treat each other on social media? Who holds power in the congregation and for how long, and who doesn't? Compare what you observe to the good news. What's incongruent? What are one to three theological words to describe what God most hopes for them? Moving from incongruity to congruity through the lens of theology is your theological sermon arc.[1]

Consider this further. Theologically, where do they "live" now? Where is God calling them to go? Be watchful, aware, tuning your senses to the harmonic resonances of the Spirit, and notice if they are changing. What do you see?

In addition to considering how to use the bully pulpit to apply the force, time, and distance of words, be cognizant of the thoughts, beliefs, and behaviors that would have to shift if the congregation moved toward a new theological landing place. For example, imagine the Corinthians. Paul wrote his first letter to tell them (in chapters twelve and thirteen) that they were getting "love" all wrong. What behaviors did he hope to see from those who loved each other as Christ loved them? The theology of love, Paul wrote, is demonstrated by acts of kindness and patience, but not by jealousy, arrogance, or rudeness. The Corinthians needed to die to self. They needed to give up their identity of being first, best, and most—and making

90

certain everyone knew it—in order to live in concert with the gospel of love.

Choose a theological theme that moves your people toward the gospel, and preach it over time in sermons and everywhere else: newsletters, off-the-cuff prayers, Bible studies, and weekday homilies. Most of all, watch your own actions so they're congruent with the theology you're preaching; that will preach most forcefully of all.

3. Know what you're talking about.

We don't have to be experts on every topic, and who could be, anyway? The complexities of applying the gospel of love of God and neighbor to climate change, racism, human sexuality, forgiving those who have caused grave harm, and creating justice out of unjust systems boggles anyone's mind. Just the same, when preaching on challenging subjects like these, we need to have done our homework and examined more than one source. Why? Obviously so we're spreading the truth, but also to build trust. People put more faith in us when we're reliable and consistent truth-tellers, and when we admit we're not the experts.

Building trust happens even more when we preachers don't like the facts; that is, when the facts don't support our personal ideas, beliefs, or the image of systems of which we are a part. This messes with our own self-identity; pieces of our own sky might fall. In our sermons we need to acknowledge the other sides of coins, the contradictions and objections, even though we don't like them.

It's also a great chance to learn from members of your congregation or people in your area who could shed light. Before

I moved to Texas, I naively saw rising oil prices as a bad thing, and falling oil prices a good one. Having lived now among many whose livelihoods depend on the cost of a barrel of oil, I see the impact on families—and many philanthropic organizations—when the price drops. Like all things, there's always more to the story. When dealing with complex issues, we need to share a nuanced story. We don't have to become experts, but we need enough solid ground of knowledge under our feet to know others' perspectives and acknowledge them. It spreads truth, builds trust and relationships, and makes people feel seen.

4. Make the invitation to transformation an actual invitation, not an agenda.

We preachers need to be clear in our hearts and minds about our convictions. We have to feel confident about the direction we believe God is calling us, even if we're not sure how to get started. We have to know deep in our souls death is necessary for new life. That's what gives us the moral and gospel courage to invite people to let their skies fall when they don't want to.

As mentioned before, we are trying to persuade listeners to hear God loves and forgives, and is more empathetic than they think is possible. We want them to accept God's invitation to accept all this and more because we believe it's in their best interest. We want them to accept the invitation to believe the good news because their lives will be transformed to become more like Christ.

However, when we offer the gospel, listeners don't want to hear us extending an invitation with all the sincerity of an invitation issued in "air quotes." This would be as genuine as the invitation a mom extends to her young daughter when she says,

"I have an idea! Would you like to go with me to the doctor's office today to get lots and lots of shots? You want to grow up strong and healthy, right? Come on, it'll be fun!" Vaccinations are in her daughter's best interest. But it won't be fun. And by her mom's tone, the daughter knows she isn't really being given a choice.

We want to persuade our listeners to accept the invitation. But if we extend the invitation in language that sounds like it's not a genuine choice but a *fait accompli*, or "the right way is my way," it's disingenuous. People will smell the agenda not from a mile away, but from uncomfortably nearby, making it all the more offensive because it's coming from the pulpit. For example, "This congregation is going to close its doors if we don't get more people in. Those who want to save this church are invited to go door to door to ask people to join." This invitation suggests there's a litmus test for those who want to save the church. Anyone who chooses not to go door to door clearly isn't interested in saving it. The sermon carries a predetermined outcome. This isn't so much an invitation as a loyalty test.

Or—true story—when I was in college in the 1980s, about fifteen students and I lived in our college campus ministry. During the summer when we were away, unbeknownst to us the chaplain made a decision. To protest and bring attention to the US involvement in El Salvador and Guatemala, he preached that our campus ministry would become one of the first national sanctuary sites to house illegal refugees, publicly and flagrantly, from those countries. The sanctuary program was new, and the legal consequences to those housing refugees were unknown. However justifiable the goal, when we students returned that fall to discover this surprise, we were not given the opportunity to study the issue, weigh the potential consequences, and then decide whether to offer our informed consent. Instead, our sky had been torn down, remodeled, the new paint color chosen, and we were "invited" to pick up a brush and be part of the program. Umm . . . not so much.

An invitation has to be genuine, no matter how good the outcome may be for us, or how congruent we believe it is with the gospel. Especially when we cannot know where people's multiple loyalties lie, or the potential losses they see that we cannot, deciding what's in someone else's best interest doesn't engender trust, it erodes it. We need to offer invitations that bolster courage and conscience but leave the decision between them and God, loving them just the same.

5. Tell stories.

Stories have a magical quality about them. Our brains are literally hardwired for them; we crave stories that have a satisfying beginning, middle, and end. We want to be drawn in, feel the drama, and then have it wrapped up so we feel that satisfying "thunk" when all the pieces land in place. Knowing this is what our brains crave, we can choose a story form that lifts up the sermon message to offer that satisfying ending. The emotional tone of the story is chosen in part based on the brittleness and transformability of the congregation: how much emotional wallop can they bear?

Brittle congregations are more likely to want stories that soothe. A brittle congregation doesn't want their feathers ruffled or to feel challenged. They're more likely to create sharper divisions about what the preacher "should" or "shouldn't" talk about from the pulpit. They want to feel assuaged and not have their opinions or perspectives challenged. (I wonder: when listeners hear a sermon they describe as "political," how often do those in agreement with the message object to that "political" sermon, compared to those who don't agree with the message?) Whether or not we give them the kind of story they want is a judgment call that behooves us to carefully discern and weigh the risks either way.

A congregation made brittle from stress is less able to take in a difficult message. If there has been a tragedy or too many internal issues, it's probably not the time to tell them a story to get them to "think." They need good news to carry them forward another day. For instance (another true story), a sermon for the funeral of a five-year-old who had been hit and killed by a drunk driver began thus: "Fifty percent of all marriages after the death of a child end in divorce." The funeral was not the occasion for that brittle congregation, let alone the grieving parents, to heed a warning about the potential death to the parents' marriage. The sermon didn't improve after that, either theologically or pastorally. In fact, when the sermon ended, the bereaved mother spontaneously stood up and told a story. She told a story about her son, their family's faith, and God. That story of faith was the good news that day, not the sermon. The quip afterward from one person in attendance was, "It was the only funeral sermon so bad it required a rebuttal."

However, when you think a congregation is able to hear a story, personalize it so people make the emotional connection to themselves. We don't change unless we're emotionally hooked, especially with empathy. I don't mean this should be done manipulatively like late-night infomercials about starving, neglected children or animals. It's when we're emotionally connected that a problem that was "over there" works itself into our hearts "right here" and becomes a call to serve.

It's also important to tell stories of the congregation's shared history, especially when a congregation is divided. Remind them of the ways God has worked in and through the congregation before and during the current period. What has the Spirit accomplished through them? What hard times have they endured? How have they come this far in their journey of faith together? What are they building together for future disciples yet to come? Write a parable to illustrate what they might still do together when they live into the Spirit's call to love God and love their neighbor—and love each other.

6. Rather than preaching issues, hold up the gospel.

What's happening in the world that you feel needs to be addressed? Immigration? Gun control? Climate change? Yes, these are all problems that require our attention. People are getting hurt; many people are not being respected; if the climate changes much more, among other innumerable disasters, a disproportionate number of the world's poor will be adversely affected.

There are two things (at least) that can trip us up when we choose to preach on such issues. The first is when we address an issue directly, listeners' ears can quickly get blocked. They might perceive we're advocating for a position that sounds to their ears not only political, but partisan. It can sound like we're offering a "right" way as opposed to others' "wrong" way of thinking. Listeners on the "wrong" side can feel defensive, shamed, and called out. To be fair, when I sense that kind of preaching, I don't listen. Do you?

The second thing that trips us up is when the issue of the day is the subject of the sermon. Our calling as preachers is not to preach about the world's issues. Our calling is to preach the gospel, and how the gospel sets the world—with its issues—to rights. The gospel doesn't call us to take a "position." The gospel calls us to position ourselves to love Jesus first and most, and tend his sheep. If we see an issue that makes the news, the issue is about people who are not being tended by others the way Jesus expects us to. The sermon needs to ask the question why: Why are they not being tended? Who and what is being loved more than these?

For example, if the issue in the news is gun control, Jesus doesn't address guns; he addresses loving God first and most, and loving our neighbors as ourselves. Jesus is interested in why someone thought it was a good idea to maim or kill the brothers and sisters they're supposed to love. Jesus is interested in our interest in the power and control the threat of gunfire infers. Jesus is interested in our desire for self-protection from others, and our disinterest in self-sacrifice for the needs of others. We don't need to preach about guns per se, but we preach the gospel that calls out what lives in the human heart: "For out of the heart come evil intentions, murder, adultery, fornication, theft, false witness, slander" (Matt 15:19).

The issues we see in the news are the symptoms of heart-, soul-, and mind-sickness. They are the behaviors of grief, fear, shame, and the fear of death. We're seeing the manifestations of actions motivated by that which does interest Jesus, to heal the diseases of the human spirit: violence, anger, greed, fear, power, shame, isolation, distrust, fractured relationships, and loving self more than God and others.

An issue in the news may serve as the message's example, but it isn't *necessary* to name the surface issue when Jesus is naming the underlying one. Describe the underlying issues of the diseases Jesus cures. If people can connect the dots themselves to the day's issues, they're prepared to hear the gospel they may not want to hear. If listeners can't connect the dots themselves, no amount of putting the gospel in their faces is going to make them more able to hear it.

7. Some have already had their fill of the cup (and then some).

We all have our losses and griefs. Each person has experienced changes and sorrows that are hard to endure. Each loss, each grief, is real, unique, and needs to be respected. When Jesus asks his disciples, including us, whether we can drink the cup he is to drink, by grace we might be able to say we are willing. We are willing to endure suffering, agony, and death for the sake of another. We offer our consent because we have the agency to consent. We are empowered to choose. We might drink that cup with gritted teeth, fear, and trembling, but we still choose. We can still guide the chalice to our lips and set the cup down after a barely detectable trace of wine has wet our lips.

Not everyone, however, gets to choose. Whole classes of peoples have had rivers of the bitter wine of loss, suffering, and grief poured down their throats by those whose hearts are overwhelmed by fear, power, and evil. We must see and acknowledge those in our pews, towns, and nation who have been shamed, isolated, and beaten down for generations: Peoples of the First Nations, immigrants, women, members of non-Christian faiths, people of color, those with mental illnesses, LGBTQIA people, and others who know too well the taste of this sour draught, the taste of being hated, reviled, feared, and persecuted. These are people who are exhausted from walking on eggshells, looking behind their backs, defending themselves, trying to fit in, and wondering whether they'll ever get a fair shake, or have the same choices the power-brokers hoard for themselves. While acknowledging individual change and losses are uniquely and painfully real, we also need to hear the truth of whole peoples who know nothing other than loss. Those, in fact, who daily are handed cups of suffering filled with wine made from rotten grapes by those who own the vineyards.

When addressing the losses and griefs of those in our pews, we need to address *all* the losses if we're going to build the reign of God. Truth-telling, lamentation, forgiveness, reconciliation, and amends are necessary between all peoples, or people will continue to foster bitterness, resentment, and enmity and we'll get nowhere. I will expand on lamentation in a separate section below. Before I do, however, I want to address the need to preach to the ones who own the vineyards.

If we are to address all people's losses as uniquely their own, this means we also have to see the losses the power-brokers will experience when the systems they have built and maintained are dismantled—and they must be dismantled if they/we are to share power. (I own both sides of the "they/we" coin. I can as much be placed among the vineyard owners for no other reason than the amount of melanin in my white skin, as I can be placed in the demographic of #MeToo.) No matter how much we preach loving our neighbors as ourselves, it is no surprise the vineyard owners resist volunteering to sip even a small, empathetic taste of the bad wine they serve others. Were they/I to do so, it would render millions of people as blind and disoriented by the truth as Saul was on that road to Damascus. Jesus's words would ring in their/my ears, "Why have you persecuted me? Remember, what you have done to the least of these, you also have done to me." They/I would see their/my roles, systems, identities, well-being, livelihoods, and relationships affected. It's no wonder the skies over their/my vineyards are so fiercely held up. If those skies weren't so highly prized, arms would have dropped and skies fallen eons ago.

I remember seeing on TV a panel of ultrawealthy adults who had inherited their money; they hadn't earned any of it themselves. When the host asked them the biggest impact their wealth had had on them, they all agreed: their wealth had given them almost unlimited choices. Their wealth had given them choices for educations and homes, travel and clothes, and even giving their wealth away if they so chose—as one panel member had actually done. Uncomfortable with not having earned his wealth, and seeing the disparity his life of choices afforded him compared to others who had not been born as fortunate, he had given his entire wealth to charities and worked for his living.

This last panelist didn't suggest he needed to apologize and make amends for anything related to his former wealth; he was born into the family into which he was born. In a similar fashion, those of us who have inherited a plethora of choices based on our skin color, gender, or heterosexuality cannot help how or to whom we were born. However, if we don't give up the disproportionate wealth of choices we did not earn, we are much like those ultrawealthy on the panel who decided not to give up their wealth. We choose daily to hang onto the systems that benefit us and exercise the plethora of choices designed to limit access to those choices by others.

We can preach a variation on Dr. Martin Luther King Jr.'s "I Have a Dream" speech. As he did, show what is possible when choices are expanded for all. What would the world look like if everyone enjoyed an equal wealth of choices? Rather than preach how necessary it is and how good it will feel to give up our choices and power and share them (which is tougher to sell), preach to emphasize the gains. Preach a vision of how great it will be for them when choices are expanded for others. For example—

I have a dream that one day the privileged will share their seats of power as easily as schoolchildren share their snacks and sandwiches.

I have a dream that one day the powerful will no longer seek to conquer our planet's resources for personal convenience and pocketbooks, but seek to catalyze our human resources to conquer our common climate crisis.

I have a dream that one day the welfare system is laid to rest because every child graduates high school, every adult reads, every health care need is met, and no one falls through the cracks in the system because no crack has survived to fall through.

What in the world do you dream of?

8. Does every sky have to fall?

Some skies deserve to fall. Some skies need to fall. Some skies will fall whether they deserve to or not. Other skies don't have to fall, and others we can't allow to fall. How do we know which is which?

For example, a sky we cannot allow to fall is the healthy remnant of our planet's climate. I can't see that melting glaciers and rising oceans that will reshape and reduce millions of miles of coastlines forcing people (mostly the poor) to move inland is loving God or our neighbors. I can't see how people dying because of intense heat waves and devastating storms is loving God or our neighbors. I can't see how continuing on our current trajectory to allow carbon dioxide levels to rise before we get to an irretrievable tipping point is loving God or our neighbors.

The litmus test is the gospel of love: are our decisions and way of life congruent with the gospel? Some decisions are clear-cut, such as doing all in our power to promote the stewardship of the earth and its inhabitants as God intends. However, the implementation of those decisions isn't as clear-cut, because improving one thing adversely affects another. For example, according to the Bureau of Labor Statistics, 6.4 million people were employed in the oil and gas industry in the US in 2017.[2] Decreasing our carbon dioxide output by using less gas will have an effect on the livelihoods of millions at all socioeconomic levels and the industries that support them. Imagine you're a forty-five-year-old hourly wage earner with children to feed, and the market for oil and gas drops. You've got more than fifteen years of experience with perks like health insurance, merit increases, and more vacation time. How excited would you be to look for another industry, move to a new place, and start again at the bottom? Would it be any wonder if those thus affected insist on holding up the skies of their livelihoods?

Whose skies should fall? Which should get propped up, patched up, and repainted? Any one situation will require its own solutions, many of which haven't been invented yet, so none of us has all the answers. What I am certain of, however, is three things for the preaching task.

First, preach God's care for all God's children, and never make one group or industry out as the "bad guys" against the "good guys." At the very least this is because, somehow, we often make ourselves out to be in the "good guy" camp.

Second, preach to call out the principalities and powers we all built together and depend on. We need to look at ourselves to confess how we contributed to creating and maintaining the systems that got us into our messes. I live in the suburbs where there's no public transportation and have to drive my gas-fueled car everywhere I go. It's not as though I have stones at the ready to cast guilt-free at my neighbor three doors down who makes his living in oil and gas. Preach to convict us all of our complicity.

Third, once convicted, preach to seek God's forgiveness, and out of gratitude for mercy received, take responsibility to make amends, even in complex, overwhelming, entrenched systems. We so often don't accept responsibility because it's easier, and far more comfortable, to give the responsibility for our systemic amendment of life to those who make the direct decisions. Rather than amend our own lives and the systems we depend on, we give them the responsibility. *They* should change it. *They* should find new jobs for people. *They* should clean up their act.

However, that's just creating a new category of "us" and "them": "we" who are now enlightened and know things need to change, and "they" who still live in ignorance, greed, and sin, and are unwilling to make the necessary changes. We create an invisible swarm of "someone else's" to clean up the mess to which we just admitted we contributed. Rather than casting new winners and losers, preach what God wants for all people. Preach the vision of shalom that includes us all, sinners and saints alike, who look remarkably like each other, and keep the responsibility for amendment of life where it belongs: with all of us.

9. Lament.

We are not good at this. We need to teach people how to grieve. We need to normalize change, death, and grief, and make it an everyday part of our lives. I recall reading about a family who had a tradition at their Friday night dinners. Each answered this question: "How did I fail this week?" It wasn't a tradition intended to publicly shame those around the table. It was done to normalize the inevitability of failure, to make sure they didn't isolate or heap shame upon themselves, and to learn from what happened. Talking about failure brought the family closer together for their shared vulnerability as they listened well, helped the speaker sort out what happened, and asked questions to help them decide what to do next. We can do this same thing if we preach about lamenting. Not every sermon, of course, but we need to comfortably preach the question, "What and how did you lament this week?"

Most of us are terrible at lamenting. We feel embarrassed by our own public expressions of grief. Our embarrassment drives us inward with shame, resulting in secret grieving with methods that are often unhealthy, causing harm and lasting longer than needed. We also don't know what to do when someone else is grieving. We feel inadequate in the face of such strong emotions, and embarrassed to witness such an intimate, heartfelt expression. Grief looks and feels out of control, and that is nothing we feel good about. In fact, how does our society describe expressions of grief? If our bodies are overwhelmed by tears, we say the bereaved "fell apart," "came undone," or "collapsed with grief." Conversely, if the bereaved is publicly stoic, we say they are "very strong" or "bearing up well." We say they'll get through the public events and "collapse later" meaning, alone and in private, where they won't bother anyone else.

A colleague-friend whom I have known for two decades helped me grieve well once. I lift her up as the example of the preaching we can offer to help our listeners lament well.

I had heard my colleague preach and witness personally to the beauty and necessity of Christian community. Moreover, she preached that being in community is often messy and inconvenient, but all the more a blessing because of it. She spoke with conviction and sincerity. I believed her, so when my moment came to grieve, she was the one I thought of.

It still took a lot of courage to dial her phone number. I pushed the first eight digits, then hesitated a full five minutes, refreshing my screen each time it dimmed. I told myself all the things we say at such moments: I don't want to be a nuisance; it's too late at night; it's not fair to dump this on her, especially someone I didn't know all that well. Still, she had built a track record of trustworthiness over the many years I had known her, and I didn't think I could bear my grief alone that night, so I finally dialed the last two numbers.

When she answered, she heard in my voice something was wrong. Fifteen minutes later, I was picked up. As soon as I was in the car, I buckled over with sobbing. She was not frightened of, nor discomfited by, my grief. She rubbed my back and told me how glad she was I had called. I was sobbing too hard to talk, and she asked no questions other than to ask what I needed: find a quiet spot for the car, or go to her home? I answered home.

When we arrived, she asked what I needed and set about meeting my requests: tissues first, water second. She settled us both in comfortable chairs. When I was ready, I lamented: a sudden change in my life had cast doubts on my livelihood, role, well-being, self-identity, and relationships. She listened. When I finished, she asked again what I needed: let the story sit, or would I like her to respond? I opted for the latter.

As we talked, the conversation shifted congenially back and forth, sometimes about me, sometimes about her. At my request, she helped me discern some immediate decisions I had to make. When I was ready, she drove me home and promised to hold me in prayer. I believed her even more than I had two hours before.

What does this event model for preaching about lamentation, both individual and corporate?

She was vocal and sincere about her willingness to help (even when messy and inconvenient): preach to be the body of Christ who is alive and active in the messy and inconvenient.

She wasn't afraid of strong emotions: preach to be filled with the courage of Christ who came at Mary and Martha's request, and stood with them while they poured out their grief with tears, anger, resentment, and accusations.

Just as Mary and Martha sent word for Jesus to come, I called and asked for help: preach the courage to trust in and ask for the help needed.

I sobbed; she waited: preach the courage not to give into curiosity, and the patience to wait as long as needed, even if it means curiosity is never satisfied.

She respected my grief to ask and respond to what I needed. She didn't presume, patronize, or sympathize: preach the gift of open-hearted hospitality that lets the bereaved call the shots.

We both accepted the blessing of vulnerability, deepening a relationship that no longer needs to be qualified as "colleague-friends"; after that, we could call each other friends: preach about the pride and shame of holding grief to ourselves because we believe it will be a burden to others, and the blessing of vulnerability that draws people together through grief shared.

Sometimes we feel if we unleash our grief, it will never stop until it does us in: preach the truth that locking away grief is what does us in, and that strength is shown when we lament, not when we hide it. Indeed, strength pours out of us when we cry, sob, talk, pray, journal, ask for help, or choose contented silence in one another's company.

Finally, "The Spirit helps us in our weakness; for we do not know how to pray as we ought, but that very Spirit intercedes with sighs too deep for words. And God, who searches the heart, knows what is the mind of the Spirit, because the Spirit intercedes for the saints according to the will of God" (Rom 8:26–27). Preach the wisdom of listening to the Spirit who knows what we need before we ask—especially when we need to lament.

10. Help listeners to wait.

That which has died is buried. That which is yet to come is unknown. And in between, we wait. If lamentation is our Good Friday, waiting is our Holy Saturday. Whether we wait with happy anticipation or in dread, I know few who possess the gift of equanimity while waiting; I am certainly not one of them.

Waiting is hard for most of us. When we are in suspense, we can feel keyed up, numb, distracted, on edge, depressed, or feel a pit in our stomach. Waiting can be harder to endure than the resolution, even if the news received is what we most dread. While waiting, our minds spin tales of disaster and worst-case scenarios, not only because we're afraid of what may come, but as a form of magical thinking. The worst things imagined rarely come to pass, so maybe if we imagine the worst, the worst won't happen. While we wait, we also pray for answers to assuage the discomfort of anxiety, for forgiveness that can lead to redemption, and for rest from the exhaustion of keeping vigil. We wait for the reversals of uncertainty to become certain, the unknown to become known, and our souls' longing to bring us to the edge of the waterbrooks.

Even while we wait, we need to let fall a piece of our skies. When we wait anxiously, we are willing something to come to an end, preferably as quickly as possible. It's as though we believe our anxiety has a power and agency of its own that can hurry things up and affect the course of the future to put us out of our misery. But, alas, our anxiety lacks such power. The anxiety and discomfort of waiting have no more effect on the outcome than a baseball player's lucky socks have on the likelihood of hitting a home run. When we surrender our self-identity as being more powerful and in control than we are, and we are more vulnerable to the changes and chances of this life than we like to admit, we find equanimity. The pit in our stomach is filled in and made whole when we surrender the false belief we can force the desired outcome, what is out of our control is in it, or that we can bring order to chaos.

Sometimes we wait with hope for an end to suffering, grief, injustice, pain, and unfairness until we wait so long we don't think of it as waiting anymore. Rather, it's just the way things are. At that point for some, hope becomes more magical than mystical. Hope is drained, for example, by injustices that are ages-old without an end in sight, and so they become accepted as deserved. For instance, a woman is sexually assaulted and we look to see what clothes she was wearing that provoked her attack; or poverty would be solved if poor people would just pull themselves up by their bootstraps. Hope is also drained with chronic illness that may continue so long we no longer remember the feeling of wholeness, so we quit looking and praying for healing. These chronic, adverse experiences gaslight us: our trust in God slowly shifts toward trusting the principalities and powers, as if they were the rulers we were supposed to have obeyed all along.

Waiting can mess with our minds, hearts, and bodies. Jesus himself seemed no fan of it. When waiting in the Garden of Gethsemane, he was grieved and agitated. Luke says his sweat fell like great drops of blood, and Jesus begged God for a way out, for a different way forward. Jesus couldn't have avoided knowing what was involved when the Romans conducted a proper death by hanging from a cross; the anticipation must have been gut-wrenching. I imagine it was almost a relief when the hour finally came and his betrayer was at hand; the agony of waiting was over.

If waiting is so hard that even Jesus had a hard time with it, what are we to preach? We can start with just that: even Jesus had a hard time with it. It's as human as it gets to suffer from waiting. Jesus empathizes with our struggles to wait, and we never wait alone.

We can preach what we fear to lose if we give to God the anxiety of waiting. Do we fear losing the illusion of control? Do we fear the truth that we have less ability to affect an outcome than we think? Do we fear discovering we really aren't God?

We can preach God's gift of ever-present hope in times of need. Hope that endures, never settles, is never complacent, and never stops imagining the world can be filled with compassion, justice, and shalom. Hope always has one more dream.

We can also preach practicing the sacredness of the present moment where God is. Being in the present is sort of like going on vacation. We escape from our worries by going where they aren't, to the present. Worrying is always future-oriented: What could happen? What might happen? We can get away from the anxiety of the future by running away to now. Now is where God has prepared the serenity of deep breaths, the luxury of giving away anxiety, and the blessed escape from our worries. Be here, be now, where God is.

The rest can wait.

11. Easter Sunday always dawns.

Waiting does end, and death never has the last word. While no one can be rushed through their grief, and it is wrong for anyone to try, we can and must preach always that there is only one thing that endures, is promised, and is here already: the good news of eternal life in Christ. No identity, role, or self-understanding can be lost when we always know our identity as a child of God; that our role is to love our neighbors as ourselves; and our self-understanding comes from being loved and forgiven. No principality or power can take these away from us. Though God knows they can and do try, they never fully succeed.

Just as the disciples met the risen Jesus several times without recognizing him, so we, too, might not recognize the resurrection in our own lives. We can be too busy looking for the resurrection we expect, instead of the one that's already here. The resurrection we expect might be a new love after our beloved dies, or a better career if our old one becomes extinct, or a new climate that's better even if altered. Resurrection might look like those, but I think there's something more fundamental we pass over. Resurrection is knowing the peace of God which passes all understanding.

Resurrection is allowing ourselves to be at peace with what is because we trust God. Resurrection is found when we grieve what we thought would come to pass and surrender what won't. Resurrection is found when we accept God's peace that makes no sense when our skies are lying in pieces all around us and we cannot see the way ahead. And yet we are at peace, because we trust that our identity as God's beloved is immutable, and the way, the truth, and the life dwells within us.

Preach this peace that passes all understanding by first praying to know it for yourself. Preach the stories of the saints whose outward and inward lives were often exquisitely difficult, yet peace-filled. They were peace-filled because they lived congruently with their conviction to love their neighbors at least as much as they loved themselves. Think of Archbishop Desmond Tutu, Mother Theresa, Harriet Tubman, and Etty Hillesum. Preach the peace that comes from dwelling in the present instead of the worries of the future, as they did. Preach the peace available when we know the only identity that matters, endures, gives us meaning, and makes sense in this world. Preach the resurrection of Christ's peace because Christ conquered death in every guise and form.

And finally, my fellow preacher, may the peace of Christ that passes all understanding keep your heart and mind in the knowledge and love of God, and of God's only begotten, Jesus Christ, now and forever. Amen.

Questions for Reflection

1. Which of these sermon approaches do you gravitate toward most naturally? Why?
2. Which of these approaches feels uncomfortable? Why?
3. Which of these approaches encourages you to take a risk in your preaching?
4. What approaches would you add to this list?

6

How to Offer
Challenging Messages

The last chapter offered eleven approaches to crafting challenging sermons. This chapter complements it with ten suggestions for how to offer them. It's one thing to figure out what to say; but how to say it is just as important.

1. Preach with empathy.

You've probably heard this before: What do realtors say is the most important feature to sell any property? Location, location, location. For preachers, the most important feature of a sermon that's heart is heard is empathy, empathy, empathy. Empathy from God and empathy from the preacher. We all need to feel seen, acknowledged, and respected, and that we're not alone. One of the most important things we can communicate when preaching challenging messages is that we as preachers struggle with the same things. There's no more powerful way to connect with someone than to communicate, "I've felt the same way."

Remember, an advantage we have as preachers is that we've been thinking about a challenging message for a while before we preach it. We've prayed about it, talked with colleagues about it, and we're clear on our theology about loving God and loving neighbor. We've done our exegesis, hit the commentaries, gone online, and maybe even attended a conference. All that time pondering, praying, and being open has moved us some distance toward the gospel. We're now ready to preach about and live it more courageously. Wonderful!

The danger, however, is not to appreciate we've traveled a long way and lose our empathy for all the steps between "there" and "here." The people who listen to the sermon haven't thought about this to the extent we have, if at all. We can easily forget all the steps and wandering through the wilderness we needed before we were persuaded to pitch our tents. If we preach about the final destination without going back to bring people along in the journey, and the time and wandering they also require, people can feel like they're on their own. They might feel we're saying there's a place they "should" be but they don't feel spiritually ready for, or they might feel ashamed they're not where we are. This might lead to feeling disconnected from God, the community, and the preacher. Sensing our empathy, on the other hand, leads to feeling the opposite: connected to God, the community, and the preacher, increasing the capacity to hear the gospel.

To help us walk alongside our listeners, remember the steps you took, and let people know you've also struggled with this challenging aspect of the gospel. I suggest keeping notes as you explore theological challenges. With each time of study or prayer, how did you feel, and what did you learn? When we preach, I'm not suggesting we describe the steps we took, books we read, or conferences we attended. I am suggesting we start back at the beginning to remember what each revelation felt like. Readily admit the struggles, or that you're still not certain. Say you're working this out, or this is a really hard thing, or you don't want to think about this either. Confess you're not eager to face the changes the gospel is asking of us, or you think you know what the gospel calls us to be, but like your listeners, you don't know how to get there either. Communicating an authentic "me too" will avoid the spiritual shock of asking people to leap from where they are over to the gospel's new coordinates you've drawn. Preaching "me too" fosters companionship that we're all part of the group of gospel explorers.

Anytime we feel like someone is in the muck with us, that we're connected by the struggle itself, it's easier to consider the next step together.

2. Angry prophetic sermons.

This is a tough one. I'm going to start with what I think is the most important thing we can do before preaching a prophetic sermon: pray a lot. Pray for wisdom and humility. Pray for clear-sightedness and wholeheartedness to see your listeners and love them to the end. Pray for empathy and pure motivation to proclaim the gospel as a servant, not an overlord. Pray for the courage to call out the powers that corrupt and bind without shaming those who have corrupted and bound—including yourself. Pray to know the grace of God who forgave you, and bring that grace with you.

Anger is tricky. Anger limits our capacity to imagine there's more to the story than we've seen so far. It puts blinders on us that limit our peripheral vision, and narrows it to the offense in front of us. We can mistake our narrow band of truth for righteous indignation, not get curious to learn the whole story, and end up shaming, and losing empathy and connection. We can mistake the virtue of humility for the sin of pride, believing we know "the truth, the whole truth, and nothing but the truth." Anger can also sound patronizing and scolding, sometimes even accompanied by shaking index fingers that say, "Shame on you." I don't know about you, but that's never worked on me; rarely, I suspect, does a "holier-than-thou" sermon convert anyone.

Anger is also tricky from the pulpit because it can sound like it's "our" thing, that we have an agenda, that we're using the pulpit like a bully in the pulpit to vent our spleens about personal injuries. Listeners can feel we're making much ado about nothing, and it's not as bad as we're describing. Especially challenging is preaching a prophetic sermon to promote God's justice for a group when we are part of the group. For example, when women preach about how women have been held back, or a gay person preaches about how gay people have been targeted for abuse, or people of color preach about systemic injustices, listeners who are not members of those groups can quickly dismiss the sermon—and the preacher. I suspect shame and fear is what most blocks the ears of listeners, but regardless, any dismissal makes it harder to hear the gospel.

Anger is also tricky because from some preachers, anger isn't acceptable. As a white woman, I know this is true for many of us; others would have to tell me their experience. When white women get angry, we're called shrill, bossy, abusive, emotional, or hysterical. When white men (all men?) get angry, they're strong, commanding, and leading. White women are expected to be polite and helpful, so if our anger is interpreted as strong, rude, or self-serving, we're called b****es. When white men are strong, rude, and self-serving, they're called leaders. For white women, then, being angry in the pulpit is a calculated risk, and the anger needs to be crafted into the sermon with extra care and clarity of purpose. I'm not saying this is fair or right, and you might accuse me of pandering to cultural norms. However, my concern in this book is how to preach a challenging message *so it's heard.* As is true for *all* of us, anger needs to be discerned for its use as the best rhetorical device for any one sermon that will help persuade people to accept a gospel they don't want to hear. We can take up complex questions about anger as its own worthy topic another time.

That's my list of concerns about angry, prophetic sermons. If you're going to use anger, as suggested above, first know why you're using it, and be able to justify it to yourself and two listeners before you preach it. This lets you double-check to be sure this really is about the gospel and not about you. If it is about the gospel, then keep the anger focused on the evil that is taking us away from the gospel of love, not on the individuals who are exercising the evil. Focus on the effects of that evil, and on those who are not being loved and respected as God declares they ought to be. If absolute power is corrupting absolutely, show us how, when, and where it is messing with hearts and minds to put a roadblock between us and the gospel. Describe the systems and their impact on people's spirits, lives, and choices. Show us the human conditions in which we are all complicit, so it's not "us" versus "them." In addition, people who have created and maintained those systems have to have a way back into community, to have open the possibility of forgiveness and redemption. If our sermons don't provide a way home, we're condemning them to an ecclesial death penalty.

117

Finally, name God's compassion and mercy for all people, so it is always love, the love of every neighbor—the righteous and the unrighteous alike upon whom God sends the rain—as the gospel message. Sermons that use anger with passion and compassion are both prophetic and pastoral. That combination makes it more likely to be heard.

3. Be authentic and vulnerable.

Another tricky one. Where's the line between authentic and vulnerable, and too much information?

Jerry Seinfeld, on his series *Comedians in Cars Getting Coffee* made an observation about the shifting subject matter for stand-up comics. Back in "his day," comics didn't talk about themselves as new, younger comedians are doing today. Jerry's generation didn't disclose conversations with their therapists, or reveal intimate details about their family of origin or ancestry. Jerry found the current trend of self-revelation off-putting to say the least.

I feel like preachers are beginning to ask similar questions. Many of us learned during our training that the preacher is supposed to get out of the way of the gospel. We're supposed to allow the gospel to be expressed with as little personal interference as possible. In my first book, *Backstory Preaching: Integrating Life, Spirituality, and Craft,* I argue that's just plain impossible. The only vessels the gospel has available are our persons and all that made us. Moreover, God asked us to preach with our unique families, experiences, personalities, and relationships with God in order to proclaim and interpret the gospel; these are what compose our backstories. Our backstories explain why ten preachers preaching to the same congregation and assigned the same passage will preach ten different sermons. Rather than get out of the way of the gospel, I believe we need to develop our backstories and place them in service of the gospel to reveal God's glory as only each of us can.

However, that's not the same thing as telling personal stories. I will never advocate for preachers to reveal the intimate details of their therapy sessions, personal details about themselves or anyone else, or talk about themselves to advance a personal agenda. What I will advocate, however, is to reveal our humanity in service to the gospel. I will advocate for being authentic and vulnerable when we don't want to hear the gospel's challenge any more than our listeners do.

For example, the night of 9/11, I called for a special service for the congregation I served. I was two days past my due date with our first child and would go into labor later that night. In part of the sermon, I used my fears regarding the vulnerability of our pending newborn and the shock of this new world I never imagined he would inherit as the dream catcher, if you will, for all our fears and vulnerability. However, the sermon concluded with a world in which we give thanks always and everywhere because Jesus Christ has conquered death and every evil.

Believe me, it took a while to get to that message of thanksgiving. It was a stretch that night for me to believe what I was saying. I wanted a gospel that gave me permission to go into full mama-bear protection mode and let me swipe my grizzly claws at anyone who dared come near my baby. I did not want to preach a gospel about love.

The vulnerability of our emotions, our honesty about not knowing what to do next, and our uncertainties and learning curves as we are in the midst of new challenges while we stand on shifting sands make the gospel message real rather than theoretical. When we admit our reluctance, fears, and struggles and still find our faith in God renewed and strengthened, the gospel enters real life where it matters. The gospel becomes relevant when listeners can see its application to our hearts as they are, and not just how our hearts might become.

In addition, we preachers become more approachable. People won't feel as reluctant to share what's really on their hearts and minds knowing we also wrestle. By naming our own vulnerabilities, we normalize others' vulnerability so they don't feel isolated; they know there's a safe person with whom to reveal their struggles.

We don't need to go into personal detail to preach authentically and vulnerably. We can use our genuine reactions to a gospel we don't want to hear either, to normalize and humanize our common struggles with it.

4. Humor.

Humor can illuminate human foibles and absurdities, and it can lighten the mood of a sermon just enough to let people hear the hard stuff. Before I offer my suggestion about using humor, here are my two don'ts about humor in the pulpit. Number one, don't routinely tell a joke at the beginning of the sermon if it's not in service of the gospel, because (number two), it highlights the preacher as comedian instead of proclaimer of the gospel. If the joke doesn't serve a direct purpose to lead listeners toward the gospel that day, it has no more purpose than that adorable story about your Aunt Marge's cat. If you're looking for a way to get people's attention and "warm up the crowd" to hear the message, then there are more effective ways to craft an introduction that accomplishes both.

The suggestion I offer comes from the Rev. Sarah Condon, who uses humor in many of her sermons. She suggests watching stand-up comics in person, or from recordings readily available on internet streaming services. Stand-up comedians deftly weave tragedy with absurdity, sorrow with the ridiculous, the unforgivable with a way out. There's a lightness with which they hold very heavy things without (when done well), cheapening or disrespecting the pain.

Good stand-up comics are also masters at getting at the essence of universal human conditions. They may tell a story that on the face of it has no connection with us whatsoever—like that adorable story about their Aunt Marge's cat—and yet, because they get to the core, we see ourselves in their story, and then their story becomes our story. A truth we hadn't recognized about ourselves is brought out and placed in our hands. We hold up the truth to the light of the comic's bit while the truth gets hotter and hotter until we want to drop it, but then the joke is made. The humor cools the truth down just enough so we're able to hold and examine the truth a little longer.

Watch stand-up comics. Take notes on how they reveal the tragic-comic overlap, and the human conditions the comics reveal. What did they do? How did they introduce the topic? What absurdity got you laughing? Follow comedians' leads to preach the comic element about the human condition the gospel reveals.

5. Prepare your listeners.

If a loved one has something difficult to tell you, how do you want to be told? Do you want to be greeted at the door with bad news blurted out in a rush before you can set down your backpack and take off your coat? Or would you prefer to have your loved one exercise a bit more restraint by waiting until you're in the door, then build up to the news by recounting the events that led to it? Or maybe you'd prefer something in-between. Regardless, you probably have a preferred process to receive difficult news, and if your loved one is sensitive, he or she will honor this so you feel as prepared as possible to hear what needs to be said.

The same is true for challenging sermon messages. Sometimes it's helpful at the beginning of a sermon not to let listeners know you're taking them to a difficult topic so you can prepare them to hear what's coming. For example, I preached a very challenging sermon and started off describing a *Calvin and Hobbes* comic strip. It got people to laugh, but like many *Calvin and Hobbes* comics, this one made a point. I carried the point forward generically with a basic application to love one's neighbor in a way no one would disagree with. Once that was established, I applied our mutual agreement to a challenging social injustice where people were not being loved as their neighbor. I received plenty of angry comments afterward, but clearly, people had listened, which is as much as I could hope for. I felt I had done my job and been faithful to my calling to proclaim the gospel. Had I started off the sermon by blurting out where we were headed, I'm confident many would have walked out and not heard the gospel that day.

In other words, get people ready to hear news they don't want to hear by following the construction of Jesus's parables. Jesus doesn't start by telling his listeners what the parable is about. He draws them in first with the twist and point revealed only at the end. Which Pharisee would have listened to the story of the good Samaritan if the Pharisee knew at the beginning of the story a Samaritan was about to teach the Pharisee a very uncomfortable lesson?

Wending our way into a challenging subject can prepare people for the "big reveal" ahead. For example, introduce the sermon with a story that makes your point obliquely (as I did with the comic strip), or rewrite the Bible story in a modern context. The latter is often especially helpful to get across the shock value Jesus's parables carried with his audience.

Or, unpack the stories of the people in the Bible we gloss over because we hear their names so often. For instance, we casually talk about Matthew the tax collector, or St. Paul the Pharisee, without often articulating their brutal histories. In a similar fashion, we often don't tell the stories of the systems in place during biblical days, like what it was like to live under Egyptian or Roman occupation. By choosing people or a piece of history that reveals systems, we can slowly draw the parallel to the systems of today.

Prepare people, then, by not showing your hand too quickly. This also means if you use sermon titles, give a title that points toward the message or asks a question, but doesn't give away the conclusion. Getting people guessing is a great way to keep them listening.

6. Select first, second, or third person for your sermon.

You probably remember your grammar lessons: first person is "I," second person is "you," and third person is "he, she, or they." Each has its advantages for adjusting the listeners' emotional distance while hearing a challenging message.

Speaking in the first person can take a difficult message and allow listeners to watch your journey to find your conclusions—without requiring them to take on the same view. It can demonstrate the preacher's personal perspectives and experience, their determinations up to this point, and where they hope to investigate next. It displays vulnerability in sharing a personal exploration of questions, doubts, mistakes, and faith, as well as humility for the preacher to show him- or herself to be a student of the gospel still.

Preaching in the first person gives the listener a bit of distance from the message. They can test for themselves the ideas that persuaded you without committing themselves to accept the same. They watch you take the hero's journey to start in one place and arrive at another, and can decide for themselves whether to make the same journey. A first person point of view trusts and respects listeners to arrive at their own conclusions, which might not be the same as the preacher's.

I did this when I preached the night of 9/11. I offered my sermon in the first person, letting them see my (vulnerable) journey from one place (fear), to another (thanksgiving). I chose the first person because I couldn't know how 9/11 was affecting my parishioners. Perhaps some had lost loved ones that day or, frankly, might have harbored prejudices against Middle Easterners or Muslims that was showing up as anger or resentment. The congregation was brittle with shock, grief, and fear, so it wasn't the time for a "teachable moment." By watching me, it gave them some distance from their own losses in light of a gospel of love. Listeners watched my journey and understood it was mine; it didn't have to be theirs. By watching me make my journey, I showed one path consistent with the gospel. I hoped it served as an example for what their journey might look like, but respected it was theirs to take. I knew with God's help they could decide for themselves what their journey would be.

Between first, second, and third person, preaching in the third person creates the greatest amount of distance between the subject and listeners. Listeners watch others take the hero's journey. They see how someone else, most likely someone they haven't met, managed the twists and turns. Listeners learn from others' mistakes and decisions. Any time we tell a story about someone like Mother Theresa or Dr. Martin Luther King Jr., we use the third person. For example, we might preach, "Mother Theresa served the poorest of the poorest of the poor. How did she do this for decades on end—especially when she felt no connection to God?" Preaching in the third person allows the protagonist to reveal hard truths and hopeful possibilities, and the preacher merely serves as the messenger. If listeners complain, we can suggest they take up their argument with God and the people in the example, since you were just the reporter. (We can also suggest, "Since this struck a nerve, maybe you'd like to talk sometime?")

Finally, preaching in the second person eliminates any emotional distance because the listener is the actor in the story. The listener takes the hero's journey making it a personal encounter with the gospel. Using the second person also gives the preacher an opportunity to tell a personal story without talking about him- or herself. We can take our own story, find the essence and purpose for telling it, then revise it in the second person to bring the listener into the action. Likewise, we can do the same with anyone's story. Using the second person is most effective when the listener is part of the action but not necessarily the conclusion. We want to help them experience the gospel using all five of their senses, but let them draw their own conclusions and applications.

For instance, if my sermon is about the humility required to change one's mind and heart, I might rely on the essence of Saul/Paul's story. I could rewrite his story in the second person so listeners experience what it's like to be converted. For example, I might start it this way.

"Imagine you're in high school. You're the president of a student club called 'Traditions.' Its mandate is to pass along the school's beloved three-century-long school traditions. However, there's a group of kids who formed a new club called 'Traditions-Renewed.' They've taken the school's cherished traditions and updated them. The twists are kind of cool (you reluctantly concede), and they are attracting attention. What disturbs you, though, is that some kids in Traditions-Renewed are asking kids who are members of Traditions to join them—and they are! By ones, and twos and fives, they're leaving Traditions to join Traditions-Renewed. What if this continues? What if the membership of Traditions is decimated on your watch?

"You're scared about the future of your club, so you ask the advice of the past three Traditions presidents: Is it acceptable to take on a new mission to destroy Traditions-Renewed by any means possible? To your relief, they give you their blessing. The next day you start a smear campaign on social media targeting the leaders of Traditions-Renewed: Lives will be ruined."

In this case, rather than watch Saul/Paul be the actor, the listener is the actor and experiences the drama. It's a much closer-to-the-heart journey. If you want listeners to experience the gospel right then and there, preach some or all of the sermon in the second person.

To summarize, decide how close to, or far from, the message you believe listeners need to be in order to hear it. The furthest distance is best created in the third person, so they watch the actor from afar. Mid-distance is first person as they watch you. The closest is second person when listeners encounter the gospel themselves.

7. Dos and don'ts.

Do:

* Speak from the heart of the topic out of your prayers and deepest beliefs.
* Develop empathy by considering multiple stories, loyalties, and competing points of view during your sermon prep and in conversations with listeners.
* Select the timing and process to name the elephants in the room.
* Drive up anxiety when gospel needs are urgent, or need to become urgent; turn it down when the anxiety is too high to be productive.
* Hold your convictions lightly: think of them more as trial runs always being tested, rather than finished products.
* Keep the responsibility to solve problems on everyone, not just leaders.
* Mix up your approaches. If you usually preach inductive sermons, preach a deductive one. If you usually preach compassionately, add a little hellfire and brimstone. If you usually preach loudly and assertively, preach quietly so people have to lean in to hear you. Offer some "head" sermons and some "heart" sermons. The point? Don't let your preaching become predictable. People will listen more when they don't know what's coming.
* Go into a challenging sermon with curiosity about how listeners react. This will teach you about the brittleness or transformability of the congregation, give you personal emotional distance, and help you craft more effective sermons down the road.

* If the sermon suggests sacrifices are necessary, make your own sacrifices public so people know you're not asking them to do something you're not willing to do yourself.
* Vet challenging sermons with trusted members of the congregation before you preach them.

Don't:

* Patronize, ignore difficult messages because they are uncomfortable, or lecture.
* Become overly invested in your convictions lest you become unable to change them, or they become too tied to your personal identity.
* Solve problems on behalf of the congregation.
* Compare one era to another, or one group to another, if the purpose is to show one was, or is, worse than the other. If we end up on the "worse" side, it makes us pity ourselves or feel like victims. If we end up on the "better" side, we may feel relieved and sympathetic we aren't as bad off as someone else. Neither is useful.
* Try to talk people out of their experiences. Only they get to say how good or bad something is or was.

8. Craft your challenging sermon like a musical composition.

Even if you're not a musician, you can think of your sermon as an orchestral composition. Consider:

What instrument best sounds like the tone of the message? Oboe: piercing and poignant. Cello: mellow and haunting. Flute: lilting and mischievous. Base fiddle: foundational and unassuming. Trumpet: Attention-getting and confrontational.

What tempo does the message feel like? Slow and steady? Normal with bursts of speed? Or a quick pace that gets the foot tapping?

What does the composition evoke? Agitation? Frustration? Mystery? Solace? Amazement?

We can make our sermon match the tones by considering the overall composition of the sermon as well as the sections.

For example, if you want the sermon to challenge long-held assumptions with a prophetic voice, the sound of your voice might be louder, demanding attention like the sound of a trumpet. Overall the pace might be quicker than you normally preach, but with sections that both slow down and mellow, setting down the trumpet to pick up the French horn, so you're not wearing people out with stridency.

Or if the message is lament, the cello might be the perfect choice. Your voice is slow, gentle, and quiet, but with bursts of a quicker pace so you don't put people to sleep.

Is the challenging message people are loved beyond measure, a message they dare not believe? Then maybe the flute so people don't take themselves too seriously; they're ready to play and dance, and when they get tired, lie in the grass to watch the clouds roll by. Your voice is light, quick, rising and falling, shifting the tempo faster and slower.

In addition, you're the soloist, so you get to choose where you play your instrument. Will the music lend itself better as a formal recital with every note purposeful and rehearsed, leading the listener in a seamless narrative from start to finish, telling one complete story? Do you want all eyes on you without distraction, and the authority a spotlight provides? In this case, your sermon might best be prepared as a manuscript and offered from the pulpit.

However, you might also be playing jazz with improvisations. You're clear on the theme, and you know whether the music is intended to console or agitate. You know where you're starting and where you want it to end, but the middle will be discovered in the moment. This sermon might better be offered standing first in front of one row of pews, then walking over to stand in front of another. It might even be helpful to move to the back so people hear the message coming at them from behind. (A tip if you're going to preach like a wandering minstrel, though: once you get to your spot, stand still and put your arms at your sides until you use your hands to gesture for emphasis. Don't make people work to follow you around the room.)

Consider your sermon as an orchestral composition to help you hear the tone and tempo your challenging message needs.

9. Normalize "the other."

The TV franchise *Star Trek* has been an extraordinary example of a narrative with a buffer to tackle difficult topics. The franchise created emotional distance for the viewer by putting the plot far into the future. *Star Trek* was one of the first (if not the first) to show that an evolved humanity would have greater equality between people of different races, genders, and species. They didn't make a big deal about it; they just wove various peoples and relationships into regular plot lines. By making these relationships ordinary and unremarkable, the imaginations of viewers were opened to imagine the same possibilities in our day.

Many sermon messages are challenging because the message asks us to welcome and include others who are unfamiliar to us; and because they are unfamiliar, people feel suspicious. People may feel threatened by these strangers' hidden agendas or motivations; the strangers might pull down a valued piece of sky. Help people get familiar. Regularly, in every context—including sermons, Christian education, newsletters, and prayers—use examples and language that uphold the dignity of others—their cultures, gender identities, sexual orientation—and use multiple ways to refer to God beyond male-gendered terms.

That said, this can't be tokenism either. Tokenism is paying lip service to inclusion, welcoming, respect, and hospitality. It's a disingenuous, insincere way to make oneself appear to value all people of God when we don't mean it. For example, if the only sermons offered that have anything to do with African Americans are in February during Black History Month, that smacks of tokenism. If all people in a diverse neighborhood are invited to church, but the new people are never offered a seat at the decision-making tables, the invitation would seem to be motivated by something other than a genuine welcome and gratitude for all God's children.

Ask parishioners to make a parish inventory. Look at the books in the parish library and the Christian education materials for children, youth, and adults. Do they represent the whole of God's people, or only a narrow slice? In gatherings, are the viewpoints of the non-majority members welcomed and freely expressed? Are accommodations made for those who are differently-abled, like giving those who might need an extra minute to find their page in the hymnal before the music begins? Are people asked the name and pronoun they wish to be addressed by, and are those wishes honored? Is God addressed in ways in which people would recognize themselves as an expression of that aspect of God's image?

At the heart of it is hospitality: making sure every person knows they are seen, welcome, and belong. In and out of the pulpit, create an environment in which the range of God's image, expressed in countless human forms, is appreciated so strangers can become friends.

10. Beyond the sermon.

Change takes time and multiple go-rounds for it to sink in, stick, and become the new normal. A challenging gospel needs a wide variety of approaches over a long period of time for us to accept and live by it. Preaching in a congregation, which reaches the most people the most often, is only one place to help people wrestle with the gospel. A comprehensive approach is often needed to tackle more complicated and emotional messages.

One of the most important things we can do in the sermon is invite people to meet with us after the service, during the week, or in a Christian education series.

Often overlooked is meeting with members before the sermon. Do a Bible study with them; ask them their thoughts and how they arrived at their perspectives. What experiences led them to their conclusions? What do they worry about? What do they hope for? What is the gospel calling them to be, do, and understand? What's the role of forgiveness, patience, and mercy in our world; are these limited? Is there anyone outside the bounds of God's love? Is there a sermon series they'd like to see and help develop?

Invite colleagues to help wrestle with difficult sermon topics; how have they handled them? How do they see the gospel calls us to love God and neighbor when applied to injustices, the stewardship of the earth, and the many changes they see coming down the pike? Would a pulpit exchange afford the opportunity for another preacher to offer the challenging sermon you believe the congregation needs to hear, but wouldn't hear as well coming from you?

What about those in authority over you? Consider bishops, canons, district supervisors, and rectors: Who has your back, and also, who do you fear would throw you under the bus? How does their support, or lack thereof, influence your capacity to offer challenging messages? Does their level of support expand or contract your capacity?

Take into account the many opportunities, support, and hindrances outside the pulpit that will help or temper your ability to offer a consistent message over time.

Questions for Reflection

1. Which of these suggestions do you gravitate toward most naturally? Why?
2. Which of these suggestions feels uncomfortable? Why?
3. Which of these suggestions encourage you to take a risk in your preaching?
4. What would you add to this list?

CONCLUSION

Challenging sermons are emotionally challenging for us to offer; they will cost us. They will cost us in the energy required to deal with people's responses; the constant discernment over which, how, and when challenging messages should be offered; and by the gospel's challenge to our own skies that need to fall. Making the time and emotional effort to preach the challenging sermons needed will require a disproportionate amount of self-care. I suggest thinking of self-care in two loose categories: self-compassion and surrender.

Self-Compassion

Preaching challenging sermons is hard because it's going to stir up people's emotions. When emotions are stirred, people—ourselves included—don't act rationally; they're going to look for places to vent those emotions. Sometimes listeners are going to vent those emotions with you, or others in the congregation, directly, passive-aggressively, or sneaking up from behind.

If you preach challenging messages, there are going to be days when you wonder why you ever agreed to preach and be a church leader. (Not to say you may not have asked yourself that question without preaching challenging messages!) You may be tempted to consider other jobs inside and outside the church. You'll probably have days you feel worn out and sorry for yourself. You'll also probably wonder if anyone in your congregation or your denominational leaders know what you're going through, how hard this is, and why so few offer to help. Knowing this, what will you do to take care of yourself? Do you already have a nonnegotiable plan of self-care you actually follow? I sincerely hope so. What does it include? I hope it includes a combination of the following:

* prayer
* sacred reading
* spiritual direction
* therapy
* peer support group
* peer sermon group
* allies (people you count on for truth-telling inside the congregation)
* colleagues (people you count on for truth-telling outside the congregation)
* exercise
* healthy eating
* regular and full vacations
* annual spiritual retreat
* continuing education
* hobbies that get you into a "flow" away from work
* self-talk with respect and care about how hard this is; cheers for doing your best; and that you really can leave work at the end of the day when there's still some "day" left in it
* self-soothing practices when listening to venting listeners
* practice of perpetual prayer
* practices to sort your own losses and multiple loyalties, like journaling, art, or other media

When you look at that list, what do you feel? Like there's nothing new here? That's the best reaction I could hope for, because it means you know what you need to do, and I hope you have your practices established. I would be thrilled if that list were the most boring part of this book for you.

Or does that list give you a sense of relief someone is giving you permission to take deep care of yourself? If so, that's another great response. Consider yourself getting permission!

Or does that list feel overwhelming and impossible? If it does, that's also good, because now you know what's required to mitigate the inevitable cost of preaching challenging messages— or pay an inflated price. If you don't mitigate the cost, the cost will be unnecessarily high, perhaps in ways destructive to yourself or others. We're all vulnerable.

When you care for yourself you are doing what Jesus commanded. You are tending one of his flock, feeding one of his sheep: you. If you don't have a self-care practice already, I urge you to create one and practice it vigilantly. A habitual practice of self-compassion will be your best friend, because when you're in the midst of preaching challenging messages, your practice will carry you.

Surrender

Challenging sermons are as authentic and effective as we have engaged the challenging message ourselves. For instance, the early draft of this book started off with a very different tone. It was dry, academic, and aloof. It didn't sound like me; people who have read my previous book or blog wouldn't have recognized me. This book wouldn't have helped a whit because no one would have read it; even I was bored reading it!

After months of stress and angst, I had a breakthrough two months before the manuscript's deadline. I realized I was holding my own grief at bay over the losses I was writing about. I felt so overwhelmed by the scale of changes to come, the world my sons are inheriting that I hadn't anticipated for them, and my fear for so many of the world's poor, that I was writing at a distance to keep my grief at a distance. I was holding up a sky that couldn't be held up. When I allowed grace to show this to me, it was a small version of Saul's moment on the road to Damascus. I was ready to let my skies fall, and I did. I wept, I prayed, I journaled, I wept some more—and I was set free. I knew a lot of "Good Fridays" were in motion and many more are still ahead, but I could see Easter in the midst of them. The moment I let my sky fall, I began to rise. I found my voice for this book, and it flowed. It turned out dying really *wasn't* so bad.

One of the greatest blessings any human can receive is the blessing of surrender. It's a profound blessing to surrender ourselves to the truth that at any time our skies not only can fall, but they will. Our egos. Our dreams. Our relationships, systems, and expectations. Our jobs, nation, economy, health, and careers. Our life. Surrendering is a blessing because we no longer use all our minds, and all our strength, and all our hearts to hold up a falling sky. It is a blessing when we let our skies fall because we are freed to trust that that which falls rises again, by God's grace and mercy.

The blessing of surrender gets underway when, arms overhead, straining under the weight of our falling sky, sweat dripping from our noses, biceps and quads shaking, we let Grace, (God's grace), face us. Though she sees our distress, Grace stands relaxed, arms at her side. Our eyes are riveted to the increasing curvature or our sky, watching in horror as it droops, enthralled

138

by fear, struggling, pushing, shoving our sky back up. We tell ourselves stories of the nightmares ahead, the moment our arms drop, of losses we cannot bear, of a future that holds no hope. Our eyes glance at Grace, glaring. We are too out of breath to demand to know why she isn't helping.

Grace breathes gently, slowly. She remains, unmoving, watching our eyes frantically dart back and forth to our sky, and back to her. She stays, steadfast, until her easy breath slows our own. We become quiet, so quiet we can hear her whisper, "Do not be afraid," she says. "You are mine, and I love you. You are safe, and I will never leave you. When you're ready, you can let go."

We stand there until we let one arm down, then the other. Our sky falls. We rage, we cry, we keen our lament. Grace holds us in faith, wraps us in hope, and with us, chants the love song of our unending hymn, "I am Child of God . . . I am Child of God . . . I am Child of God. . . ."

That is the gospel we want to hear.

NOTES

Introduction

1. The Ocean CleanUp, "The Great Pacific Garbage Patch," https://tinyurl.com/y5b9o4lr.
2. Thomas L. Friedman, *Thank You for Being Late: An Optimist's Guide to Thriving in the Age of Acclerations* (New York: Farrar, Straus and Giroux, 2016).

Chapter 1

1. Categories of loss credited to Kenneth R. Mitchell and Herbert Anderson, *All Our Losses, All Our Griefs: Resources for Pastoral Care* (Louisville: Westminster John Knox, 1983).

Chapter 2

1. Those "six degrees of separation" between people? Studies show we don't have far to go to confirm we live in a small world after all. See Thomas MacMillan, "The Classic Study That Showed the World Is Smaller Than You Think," The Cut, March 2018, https://tinyurl.com/w9e4emn.

Chapter 3

1. Ronald A. Heifetz, *The Practice of Adaptive Leadership: Tools and Tactics for Changing Your Organization and the World* (Boston: Harvard Business Review Press, 2009).

2. Joan Chittister, *Scarred by Struggle, Transformed by Hope* (Grand Rapids: Eerdmans, 2003). Kindle edition, loc. 428.

Chapter 4

1. Thomas L. Friedman, *Thank You for Being Late: An Optimist's Guide to Thriving in the Age of Accelerations* (New York: Farrar, Straus and Giroux, 2016).

2. Joan Chittister, *Scarred by Struggle, Transformed by Hope* (Grand Rapids: Eerdmans, 2003).

3. *The Book of Common Prayer* (New York: Church Publishing, 1979).

4. Dani Shapiro, *Inheritance: A Memoir of Genealogy, Paternity, and Love* (New York: Knopf, 2019).

5. Chittister, *Scarred by Struggle, Transformed by Hope.*

Chapter 5

1. With thanks to the Rev. Dr. Mark Jefferson for the phrase "theological arc."

2. U.S. Department of Energy, "U.S. Energy and Employment Report," Energy.gov, 2017, https://tinyurl.com/y6wvcvd6.

ACKNOWLEDGMENTS

Thank you to those who first allowed me to experiment with these ideas, including the Rev. Vicki Hesse and the participants of the Epiphanies Conference, February 2019, and the participants in the Preaching Lab, Episcopal Church in Minnesota, the School for Formation, Spring 2019. You let me know these ideas had legs. I couldn't have been certain of, or refined the ideas without you. Thank you for taking a chance on new thoughts under construction.

Thank you to the Rev. Dr. Karoline Lewis, whose support and referral sent me to this new publishing endeavor of Working Preacher Books. Thank you as well to my editor, Scott Tunseth, for allowing this project to evolve into what it needed to be. I deeply appreciate your faith in these ideas.

Thank you, too, to those who offered invaluable feedback on the manuscript, especially Ms. Shaundra Taylor and the Rev. Terri Thorn. This is a stronger work because of your time, effort, and attention to detail.

Finally, my biggest thanks go to my husband, Erik. Were it not for his Herculean efforts to keep home and hearth intact while I was preoccupied with this project, this book could not have been written. Thank you, Erik, not only for keeping the pantry filled, but for countless cups of coffee made and brought, making sure I ate now and then, and for your unwavering support.

Compelling and timely books on biblical preaching.
Good preaching changes lives!

Working Preacher Books is a partnership between Luther
Seminary, WorkingPreacher.org, and Fortress Press.

Books in the series include:
Preaching from the Old Testament by Walter Brueggemann

Leading with the Sermon: Preaching as Leadership by
William H. Willimon

*The Gospel People Don't Want to Hear: Preaching Chal-
lenging Messages* by Lisa Cressman

A Lay Preacher's Guide: How to Craft a Faithful Sermon by
Karoline M. Lewis